Dare to Step Out in Faith

Suzanne Pillans

New Wine Press

New Wine Ministries
PO Box 17
Chichester
West Sussex
United Kingdom
PO19 2AW

ISBN: 978–1–903725–89–4

Typeset by CRB Associates, Reepham, Norfolk
Printed in Malta

Contents

About the Author

Suzanne Pillans, her husband Wilfrid and daughter Rebecca, own and run Standlake Equestrian Centre and Ranch in Oxfordshire, UK.

Suzanne's ministry *Step Out in Faith* has grown into an International Bible School for the rural parts of Africa and the Far East, as well as a Bicycle Ministry that plants churches in the most remote villages. Fifty-five evangelists planted 138 churches in the first year and twenty-eight Bible schools were set up. Suzanne also speaks in many crusades, conferences and churches worldwide and has written five books. Her last book *Dare to Enter His Presence* made the USA TV's *Harvest Show* as 'Featured Book' on 2nd May 2006.

Introduction

Reading God's Word and prayer raise one's heart and life to a new level. The teaching from the Bible fills one with increasing faith, that ushers a person forth, filled with God's glorious Holy Spirit to witness this marvellous gospel to others.

There is no higher touch, more pure, more clean, more fulfilling than the Holy Spirit. His wonderful peace and joy make one want to know our living God more and more.

This book is simply some of the marvellous truth that God has revealed to me through studying the Bible.

This has energised me into this glorious walk, where the Lord wants us all to walk.

May God bless you greatly as you read *Dare to Step Out in Faith*.

Foreword

'It is not often that I come in contact with an individual who is compelled by love and that can truly proclaim, *"In Him* [I] *live and move and have* [my] *being"* (Acts 17:28). Suzanne Pillans is not just another author; she is a woman of faith, walking in obedience to His voice and His voice alone. If you are on a quest for freedom, then read this book. Freedom is not given to those who simply desire it; it is given to those who pursue it with all their heart. Suzanne Pillans is a whole-hearted freedom fighter in the Kingdom of God. She is a forerunner in our day, with a message of faith, freedom and compassion, who carries a divine treasure of His glorious love. She walks in a level of faith that sees things from His perspective. She aches for God's people to be set free. I encourage you to read the pages of this book. It is a very dangerous book that will leave no room for passive Christianity. This is the hour that men and women of great faith must stand firm until the end for His glory. Isaiah 7:9 says: *'If you do not stand firm in your faith, you will not stand at all'* (NIV). God took time to carve this message in this messenger. Allow the words of this book to erupt within the fibres of your being and help you to walk in all He created you to be.'

Bob Deering
Founder of Voice Ministries and the International House of Prayer
Michiana Elkhard, Indiana, USA

Do Not Limit God

Is the Lord preparing us for revival right now? Can He use mere human beings like you and me to do such an incredible thing? Is He prepared to teach us how to bring about revival? The answer is 'Yes'! That's if we will listen to Him, and yield ourselves to obey Him, regardless of what we may think of ourselves.

It was in Malawi, in November 2004, that the Lord began to challenge me in a new way. This was my third visit. The first visit was to Migowi for only one believer, but the Lord always has a plan. The next morning four ladies, too sick to walk to the market, came and knocked on my door. Jesus healed all four and they ran to the market and told everybody. From these four ladies many came to our crusade and many became believers and received healing, but even more than that; the Lord answered the 400 new believers' prayer to send rain to end their devastating drought and within the hour it rained. This caused the entire community to become Christians and since then they have built a large church.

This November I was invited to speak in their new church and of all things I got diarrhoea, but I was still determined to preach. I made it to the lectern and feeling sick, dizzy and weak simply spoke what came out of my mouth. I then sat down.

'Any one sick come forward now.' Thirty rushed forward. 'Put your own hand on your sickness or your pain and when you are

*Migowi: following the healing of four ladies,
hundreds of people come to the crusade*

*Bononque Benedicroto is healed of leprosy;
he walks without crutches and all pain is gone*

healed put your hand high in the air.' Within two minutes every hand goes up. They are all healed and go and sit down.

I was then introduced to twelve pastors behind me. I had not even noticed them and one had travelled over sixty miles to hear me speak, and I cannot remember one word that I spoke! I did not feel good about this. Anyway, knowing that I was sick, they released me and I went back to the room where I was staying.

I played back the tape and was amazed to discover that it was a perfect message for pastors. How could that be?

Two days later in Blantyre I was better and it suddenly dawned on me that I was the only one who was not healed during that service! So I decided to ask the Lord about it. He replied and said, 'To cause you to rely totally and completely on Me.' Then I understood. I had been too sick to give anything of self. I had to rely on the Lord and the result was a perfect sermon, the best I've ever preached and 100% of the people there were healed, without even the laying on of hands or standing up from my chair.

> Less of me, more of Thee;
> *None of me, all of Thee.*

Then the Lord said, 'Do not limit Me. Let Me be God.'

'How am I limiting You?' I asked.

And the Lord led me to 1 Kings 18:30–40 and said, 'If Elijah had not soaked the sacrifice three times with water and filled the trench with water too, he would have limited My miracle.' Oohh!!

Yes, a high standard. I mean, if God had not answered with fire, they would have killed Elijah. Elijah really must have known God well, so well that he knew God would answer, even if he made it impossible for the sacrifice to burn. Elijah did not limit God. He let God be God, and God answered with fire and consumed the burnt offering and the wood and the stones, and the dust, and licked up the water that was in the trench, and when the people saw it they fell on their faces:

> *'Now when all the people saw it, they fell on their faces; and they said, "The LORD, He is God! The LORD, He is God!"'*
>
> (1 Kings 18:39)

In one hour Elijah had turned the nation back to God. This is the faith God is looking for, and He is looking for mere ordinary people, people like you and me. Was I able to take up this challenge? I was soon to find out.

The next crusade was down on the Mozambique border, for five days. It was very hot and at the first service fewer than twenty-five people showed up, and they were mainly women and children. Sometimes, I thought, people just don't take women seriously.

I gave the gospel and all that was going through my mind was, 'Don't limit God. Don't limit God. How?' And then I knew.

I announced, 'I want you to go out now and look for the sickest person in this community and bring her here tonight. Then I want you to invite the entire village to come and watch Jesus heal this person!' They all left to do the job.

That night the church was full to capacity, and yes they did bring the sickest person, seriously sick, not out of bed for two years. She could not walk and was too weak to stand. She was painfully thin, had sores on her body and shivered under a grey blanket. I commanded the sickness to leave her in Jesus' name. I commanded her body be healed in Jesus' name. I commanded strength come into her body in Jesus' name. I then said, 'In the name of Jesus stand up.' And she stood up. 'Now, in the name of Jesus walk.' And she walked. 'And now, in the name of Jesus run down the aisle and back.' She looked at me in horror. 'In Jesus' name you can,' I answered and she took off, running down the aisle and back, totally healed. It's easy to give the gospel when the people see a miracle like this and they praised and worshipped God until 3.00 am.

The next day the church was full and many came between services, group after group of people, to receive their healings

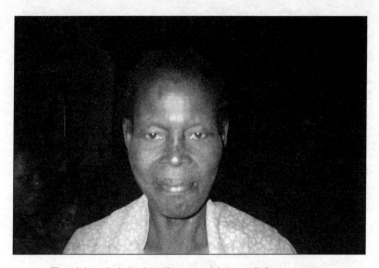

*The sickest lady in the village, unable to walk for two years,
gets up and runs down the aisle*

*Maria Homozie, born deaf and dumb, now 11 years old,
is healed and able to repeat words*

and also Jesus into their hearts as Lord and Saviour. Even two chiefs were healed and became Christians, also two girls, Judith fourteen and Maria eleven, both born deaf and dumb. Jesus healed them both and they could now learn how to speak. Judith came back two days later to show me how many words she could already say. Yes, I was learning not to limit God, to let God be God, but the Lord had much, much more to show me.

Back in England the Lord began to show me how we limit God in so many ways, by our unbelief, lack of prayer, lack of commitment and worst of all by our putting other things before Him. Then He led me to Judas in Matthew 26:15:

> ' "What are you willing to give me if I deliver Him to you?" And they counted out to him thirty pieces of silver.'

And the Lord said, 'In that moment, Judas loved the money more than Me.' Everywhere people are doing the same as Judas, loving their money, or jobs, or holidays, or homes, car, sport, lifestyles, comfort, even TV, more than Jesus. Then we wonder why the Lord is not moving when we have limited Him so much.

From that moment on I began to preach this message wherever I was invited to speak, and, to my amazement, whole churches repented every time, with many of the people in tears.

Then I felt I should go further than repentance. After all, repentance is the first step into the presence of God. So I led the people into thanking the Lord for what He had done and then to praise Him for who He is. We then came into an active, charged expectant silence. Suddenly people would sink to their knees, some flat on their faces crying. Was it us entering the Holy of Holies, the Holy presence of God, or was it the Holy Spirit coming down upon us? Or both? For suddenly, something very unexpected happened. People began to cry with joy and shake, and people were suddenly healed in their seats, set free and touched in a beautiful way.

Even in the larger churches, when we came up into the

presence of God, people were suddenly being healed all over, without any laying on of hands, no calling them to the front, nothing. Jesus had simply come down in the power of the Holy Spirit and healed them in their seats. All I did was call them forward to testify and this they willingly did, some with much emotion. Some of these healings were from sicknesses of twenty years, arthritis gone, chests healed, crippled hands loosened and healed, poor eyesight healed and many other ailments.

When we step out in faith, when we are prepared not to limit God, to let God be God, then God moves in power and answers our prayer.

He actually wants to meet with us. He actively wants to come down in power and heal the sick. But it's no use just reading the Bible without action. It's also no use praying without believing God will answer. When we read the Bible, believe the plain Word as it says, let it become part of you, then as you walk in it, the power of Heaven becomes activated through your life.

When you pray, pray believing God, pray to the living God, knowing that He is alive and hears you. Pray with expectancy and He will hear you and He will respond.

Some Questions to Think About

- Can the Lord use you to bring revival?
- Are you willing to allow the Lord to bring revival through you?
- What level of trust and faith should we aim for?
- How does reading the Bible and action come together?
- How do you know God will answer?

Rise Up to Your Potential and Calling

It is a known fact that most people *only* use 5% of their brain potential. It is also the same spiritually. Most people barely live 5% of their potential and calling in Christ.

We do not seem to realize that there is much more for us in Christ, yet somehow so many of us seem to have missed it. I know I did for many, many years. Somehow we just seem to live at the beginning stages of Christianity, having accepted Christ into our hearts, possibly even been baptised in the Holy Spirit, yet somehow we just don't seem to grow up into Christ our Head.

Whilst running the Spring Valley Holiday Farm and Riding Centre in South Africa, I noticed that in the Christian camps that came to us many Christians had come to a certain place in Christ and then gone no further. I thought to myself, 'There must be more.' At first I turned to man for the answer, but got no answer. Then I turned to the Bible and Jesus and I did get an answer.

The Bible says in John 3:31:

> 'He who comes from above is above all; he who is of the earth is earthly and speaks of the earth. He who comes from heaven is above all.'

What is this saying? This speaks of two realms, the earthly realm and the heavenly realm. This passage follows the famous passage of how Nicodemus came to Jesus at night. In John 3:3, Jesus answered him:

> *'I tell you the truth, no one can see the kingdom of God unless he is born again.'*   (NIV)

In verse 4 we read:

> *'Nicodemus said to Him, "How can a man be born when he is old? Can he enter a second time into his mother's womb and be born?"'*

Then, in verses 5 and 6:

> *'Jesus answered, "Most assuredly, I say to you, unless one is born of water and the Spirit, he cannot enter the kingdom of God. That which is born of the flesh is flesh, and that which is born of the Spirit is spirit"'*

This is speaking of two realms. Nicodemus was speaking in the earthly realm, Jesus was speaking in the heavenly realm, but at the same time He was showing Nicodemus how to live in the heavenly realm. First, he had to be born anew, or in modern language, born again of the Holy Spirit.

Now if we go back to Genesis we read:

> *'And the LORD God commanded the man, saying, "Of every tree of the garden you may freely eat; but of the tree of the knowledge of good and evil you shall not eat, for in the day that you eat of it you shall surely die."'*   (Genesis 2:16–17)

We all know that Adam and Eve ate of this tree and from that day became spiritually dead. We are born of the flesh only and we all know that all flesh has to die too. That leaves man in a very helpless and hopeless condition for eternal life. It means we shall all die in our sin, for we have all sinned, we have all fallen short of the glory of God, each has gone his own way.

But the Good News is in John 3:16:

> *'For God so loved the world that He gave His only begotten Son, that whoever believes in Him should not perish but have everlasting life.'*

The moment we receive the forgiveness of sins that Jesus made available for us by taking our sin upon Himself on the cross and receive Jesus into our hearts as Lord and Saviour we receive the Holy Spirit. The moment we become born again of the Holy Spirit we become *born again to eternal life.* We become children of our Father in Heaven, we become spiritually alive in Him: our dormant or dead spirits are made alive in Christ and become united with the Holy Spirit, whom Jesus sent to us from Heaven to dwell in our hearts. We can now call God 'Our Father', not only our Lord or our God, but our Father, who art in Heaven!! Now Jesus would not have taught us to *say*, 'Our Father, who art in Heaven', unless it was possible to get there, while we are still on earth. How? Through prayer, through abiding in Christ, by dwelling in His presence. This is what raises us above the earthly realm to live in the heavenly realm. We become whole in spirit, soul and body.

1 Thessalonians 5:23–24 says:

> *'Now may the God of peace Himself sanctify you completely; and may your whole spirit, soul, and body be preserved blameless at the coming of our Lord Jesus Christ. He who calls you is faithful, who also will do it.'*

Jesus came to save men, not just souls. He came to save the spirit from death, to give us eternal life. He came to save the soul from sin to give us peace, and the body from sickness to give us healing, even as it says in 3 John 2:

'Beloved, I pray that you may prosper in all things and be in health, just as your soul prospers.'

Now in the world we know the studies:

- *Physiology* – the knowledge of the human body and the conditions of the body.
- *Psychology* – the knowledge of the mind and its powers, speaking of the soul.
- *Pneumatology* – the knowledge of the spirit and its activities and forces.
- *Ontology* – the highest study, which is manifestations of man's body, soul and spirit.

Now God does not demonstrate mind over matter as the scientists do mentally. He demonstrates a higher fact: the power of the Spirit over mind and matter. All men are born in the flesh with a soul. Without the Spirit of God, the soul will gratify the flesh and its desires. When man is born again of the Holy Spirit he becomes spiritually alive. Now as man grows up into Christ, who is the Head, just as it says in Ephesians 4:15: *'but, speaking the truth in love, may grow up in all things into Him who is the head – Christ'*, the soul will begin to yield to the Holy Spirit, who is greater than the body, thus transforming man more into the image of Christ, until we realize that we are actively spiritual beings with a soul that dwells in an earthly body.

Firstly, putting away sin is essential for the heart of man to become one with the heart of Christ. This relationship is like a transfusion of His life and love through all our being, through the Holy Spirit coming to dwell in our beings and spirit, and then His healing to our bodies becomes as natural as His peace to our minds or His rest to our spirits declaring that Christ has become our all in all. When we receive Jesus into our hearts and are baptised in the Holy Spirit, we must not just stay in the earthly realm as so many do, but instead spend time reading the Bible

and in prayer, to bring about the renewing of our mind. Romans
12:1–2 says:

> *'I beseech you therefore, brethren, by the mercies of God, that you
> present your bodies a living sacrifice, holy, acceptable to God, which
> is your reasonable service. And do not be conformed to this world,
> but be transformed by the renewing of your mind, that you may
> prove what is that good and acceptable and perfect will of God.'*

This scripture, along with also hearing the voice of Jesus, will help
us to recognise and resist the lies of the enemy. Jesus will speak
truth to us and the truth sets us free. Then as our soul stops just
gratifying the desires of the flesh, it takes on the character of
Christ. When this happens, we stop living in just the limited
earthly realm; we begin to live in the heavenly realm instead.

Ephesians 1:3–5 says:

> *'Blessed be the God and Father of our Lord Jesus Christ, who has
> blessed us with every spiritual blessing in the heavenly places in
> Christ, just as He chose us in Him before the foundation of the
> world, that we should be holy and without blame before Him in
> love, having predestined us to adoption as sons by Jesus Christ to
> Himself, according to the good pleasure of His will . . .'*

Then Ephesians 1:16–23 says:

> *'[I] do not cease to give thanks for you, making mention of you in
> my prayers: that the God of our Lord Jesus Christ, the Father of
> glory, may give to you the spirit of wisdom and revelation **in the
> knowledge of Him**, the **eyes of your understanding** being
> enlightened; that you may know what is the hope of **His calling**,
> what are the riches of the glory of His inheritance in the saints,
> and what is the exceeding greatness of His power **toward us who
> believe**, according to the working of **His mighty power which He
> worked in Christ when He raised Him from the dead and***

*seated Him at His right hand in the heavenly places, far above all principality and power and might and dominion, and every name that is named, not only in this age but also in that which is to come. And He put all things under His feet, and gave Him to be head over all things to the church, which is His **body**, the fullness of Him who fills all in all.'* (emphasis added)

We can know God!! We can rise up in prayer to that which God has called us to. When we receive Jesus and His indwelling Holy Spirit into our lives we are born to eternal life and our spirits come alive. But there is still another level.

We can also be baptised in the Holy Spirit. This is what happened to the Apostles on the Day of Pentecost. Read for yourself what it says in Acts 1:7–8 and Acts 2:4. When we receive the baptism in the Holy Spirit we also receive the gifts of the Holy Spirit and power.

We then come to know the power of His Holy Spirit who dwells in our hearts, the same Holy Spirit who raised Jesus from the dead!! Yes, this same Holy Spirit who raised Jesus from the dead now dwells in our mortal bodies!! If only we could realize this and live it, we would come to know His great power that enables us to live and witness for Him, who is seated at God's right hand far above all rule and authority and power and dominion and above every name that is named. That is, above all evil, all sin, all sickness, all demons and every force of darkness. This is not all. Ephesians 2:1–10 says:

'And you He made alive, who were dead in trespasses and sins, in which you once walked according to the course of this world, according to the prince of the power of the air, the spirit who now works in the sons of disobedience, among whom also we all once conducted ourselves in the lusts of our flesh, fulfilling the desires of the flesh and of the mind, and were by nature children of wrath, just as the others. But God, who is rich in mercy, because of His great love with which He loved us, even when we

were dead in trespasses, made us alive together with Christ (by
grace you have been saved), **and raised us up together, and**
made us sit together in the heavenly places in Christ Jesus,
that in the ages to come He might show the exceeding riches of
His grace in His kindness toward us in Christ Jesus. For by grace
you have been saved through faith, and that not of yourselves;
it is the gift of God, not of works, lest anyone should boast. For
we are **His workmanship, created in Christ Jesus** *for good*
works, which God prepared beforehand that we should walk in
them.'   (emphasis added)

Where? In Heaven or here on earth?

The Bible speaks of this happening now and in the coming
ages, while we are still on earth, that we should walk in them
now. Jesus wants to raise us up above sin, sickness and all
demonic powers and raise us up with Himself into the heavenly
places. When we live in the limited earthly realm, sin is a struggle,
sickness is stronger than us, demons, curses, evil spirits and all
demonic things are stronger than us, but when Jesus raises us up
with Him into the heavenly places, He raises us up, above sin,
above sickness and above every demonic thing, into His victory.

Then He gives us the authority of His name to cast out
sickness, to cast out pain, to cast out demons, as it says in Mark
16:17–18:

> *'And these signs will follow those who believe: In My name they will*
> *cast out demons; they will speak with new tongues; they will take*
> *up serpents; and if they drink anything deadly, it will by no means*
> *hurt them; they will lay hands on the sick, and they will recover.'*

In Luke 10:19 it says,

> *'Behold, I give you the authority to trample on serpents and*
> *scorpions, and over all the power of the enemy, and nothing shall*
> *by any means hurt you.'*

How can this be? Philippians 2:8–11 tells us:

> *'And being found in appearance as a man, He humbled Himself and became obedient to the point of death, even the death of the cross. Therefore God also has highly exalted Him and given Him the name which is above every name, that at the name of Jesus every knee should bow, of those in heaven, and of those on earth, and of those under the earth, and that every tongue should confess that Jesus Christ is Lord, to the glory of God the Father.'*

The authority of His name that He gives to us is what enables His healing on earth. He secured this victory on the cross, and from that moment, every knee must bow to the authority of His name. When we command sickness to go in His name, it must obey, pain must obey, demons must obey, that is *if we are truly living* in the heavenly realm in Christ Jesus.

Colossians 3:1–2 says:

> *'If then you were raised with Christ, seek those things which are above, where Christ is, sitting at the right hand of God. Set your mind on things above, not on things on the earth.'*

When we seek to live in the heavenly realm in Christ Jesus, He raises us up above the earthly realm into another dimension of living in Him. To this life He has called us, for this life He has prepared us, even before the foundations of the world, that we should walk in Him.

Let us no more be limited to walk in the earthly realm, let us look to Jesus and let Him raise us up to the full potential and calling that He has **called each of us to live. We can all live in the heavenly realm in Jesus, our Lord and Saviour**.

Some Questions to Think About

- What is the difference between living in the earthly realm and living in the heavenly realm?
- How can we be lifted up into the heavenly places where Christ dwells?
- Name three areas in our lives that Jesus changes by what He did on the cross.
- What power does the authority of Jesus' name have on the earth?
- How do we receive this power and authority, to live as Jesus wants us to and to do His work on earth?

The Power of
the Cross

The very first miracle of Jesus was turning water into wine. This was a creation miracle, a miracle of creation. He also walked on water, calmed the storm and fed 5,000 people with only five small loaves and two fishes. Then, if that was not enough, He had His disciples collect twelve baskets of crumbs.

What is Jesus showing us here? He had power over creation. He also had the power to cast out demons and much of His ministry was doing this very thing. He also healed all who came to Him, healing many by His word or by laying hands on them. He also had power to forgive sin. He even had power to raise the dead and waited four days before calling Lazarus forth. Not only that, He Himself rose from the dead after three days.

What is Jesus trying to tell us?

What is the meaning of these incredible miracles?

Is there something behind all this, something each one of us needs to know?

One clue is in Genesis 1:28:

> 'Then God blessed them, and God said to them, "Be fruitful and multiply; fill the earth and subdue it; have dominion over the fish of the sea, over the birds of the air, and over every living thing that moves on the earth." '

God gave man the earth to rule over.

Psalm 8:4–8 says:

> *'What is man that You are mindful of him,*
> *And the son of man that You visit him?*
> *For You have made him a little lower than the angels,*
> *And You have crowned him with glory and honour.*
> *You have made him to have dominion over the works*
>   *of Your hands;*
> *You have put all things under his feet,*
> *All sheep and oxen –*
> *Even the beasts of the field,*
> *The birds of the air,*
> *And the fish of the sea*
> *That pass through the paths of the seas.'*

God made man ruler over the works of His hands, to be only subject to God and His love, to be in complete control over all God's creation on Earth.

What Went Wrong?

Adam and Eve ate of the fruit of the tree of knowledge of good and evil. Up to that time the earth was perfect. There was no sin. There was no sickness. There was no death. Creation was perfect. There were no weeds, no disease in the crops or animals. All that grew from the ground was perfect. What did Adam and Eve do when they ate of the forbidden fruit?

Genesis 3:13 says:

> *'And the LORD God said to the woman, "What is this you have done?" The woman said, "The serpent deceived me, and I ate."'*

The devil deceived Adam and Eve, causing them to doubt God and then to disobey Him, which is rebellion, and they ate of the

Tree of the Knowledge of Good and Evil, which allowed sin into this world that God had given to man. Sin came into the world through disobedience. This was the Fall of Man. Now sin had come into their world. The world God had created for them was exchanged for the knowledge of good and evil, as described in Romans 5:12:

> *'Therefore, just as through one man sin entered the world, and death through sin, and thus death spread to all men, because all sinned.'*

In John 14:30 Jesus says:

> *'I will no longer talk much with you, for the ruler of this world is coming, and he has nothing in Me.'*

Now the devil was thrown out of Heaven and is in rebellion against God. In Psalm 74:10–11 the psalmist prays:

> *'O God, how long will the adversary reproach?*
> *Will the enemy blaspheme Your name forever?*
> *Why do You withdraw Your hand, even Your right hand?*
> *Take it out of Your bosom and destroy them.'*

The devil is in rebellion against God and also hates human beings, because human beings are made in the image of God, as it says in Genesis 1:26a:

> *'Then God said, "Let Us make man in Our image, according to Our likeness..."'*

How can the devil take revenge against God? By taking as many people, whom he knows God loves, down to Hell with him, and how can he do that? In any way he can, by tempting man to sin. If he cannot do that he will inflict them with sickness, or curses, or attack the mind with satanic spirits, fears, or deceive them in any way he can through worldly ways, worldly thought, sects and false religions. If he cannot do that he will try to lead them away from the Bible, into complacency or through lies or any way he can.

2 Corinthians 4:4 describes unbelievers as those:

> *'whose minds the god of this age has **blinded**, who do not believe, lest the light of the gospel of the glory of Christ, who is the image of God, should shine on them.'*   (emphasis added)

Also, in Ephesians 2:1–2 we are told:

> *'And you He made alive, who were dead in trespasses and sins, in which you once walked according to the course of this world, according to the prince of the power of the air, the spirit who now works in the sons of disobedience . . . '*

This is a very interesting verse as it answers the much-asked question 'Why does God allow us to suffer if He is a loving God?' God loves man and wants us to love Him by our own free will, not like robots. He has therefore given us free choice, to choose whom we love and serve, for it is impossible to love two masters.

We have made the choice between good and evil and God only wants those of us who love Him to be in Heaven, those who have chosen to stand strong against sin and accept Him as Lord and Saviour. If we choose sin, we will receive all that goes with it and this will cause much suffering. If we choose righteousness and life, we will more ably enjoy this life on earth as well as receiving eternal life.

Deuteronomy 30:15–16 sets this out for us:

> *'See, I have set before you today life and good, death and evil, in that I command you today to love the LORD your God, to walk in His ways, and to keep His commandments, His statutes, and His judgments, that you may live and multiply; and the LORD your God will bless you in the land which you go to possess.'*

God was not happy with so many choosing to turn their backs on Him and choosing evil and death instead. Though God is greater than Satan, He cannot stoop to satanic methods in order to take back what Satan has stolen from man to give it back to man. God did not give Satan this power over man on the earth. Adam and Eve did it, and since then man has often found himself in hopeless and helpless situations.

So What Did God Do About it?

John 3:16–17 says:

> 'For God so loved the world that He gave His only begotten Son, that whoever believes in Him should not perish but have everlasting life. For God did not send His Son into the world to condemn the world, but that through Him the world might be saved.'

When Jesus walked this earth He said in John 12:30–32:

> 'This voice did not come because of Me, but for your sake. Now is the judgment of this world; now the ruler of this world will be cast out. And I, if I am lifted up from the earth, will draw all peoples to Myself.'

Jesus was speaking about the devil as ruler of this world, soon to be cast out once He, Jesus, had gone to the cross. This we will see in Hebrews 2:14–16:

> 'Inasmuch then as the children have partaken of flesh and blood, He Himself likewise shared in the same, that through death He might destroy him who had the power of death, that is, the devil, and release those who through fear of death were all their lifetime subject to bondage. For indeed He does not give aid to angels, but He does give aid to the seed of Abraham.'

It could not be plainer than that. Jesus came to save us, the descendants of Abraham, from the bondage of the devil.

In Colossians 2:13–14 we read:

> *'And you, being dead in your trespasses and the uncircumcision of your flesh, He has made alive together with Him, having forgiven you all trespasses, having wiped out the handwriting of requirements that was against us, which was contrary to us. And He has taken it out of the way, having nailed it to the cross.'*

Colossians 2:15 then says:

> *'Having disarmed principalities and powers, He made a public spectacle of them, triumphing over them in it.'*

Let us read how man was supposed to live, this time from Hebrews 2:6–9:

> *'But one testified in a certain place, saying:*
>
> > *"What is man that You are mindful of him,*
> > *Or the son of man that You take care of him?*
> > *You have made him a little lower than the angels;*
> > *You have crowned him with glory and honour,*
> > *And set him over the works of Your hands.*
> > *You have put all things in subjection under his feet."*
>
> *For in that He put all in subjection under him, He left nothing that is not put under him. But now we do not yet see all things put under him. But we see Jesus, who was made a little lower than the angels, for the suffering of death crowned with glory and honour, that He, by the grace of God, might taste death for everyone.'*

Let's look at this closely (with emphasis added):

> *'For in that He put all in subjection under him, He left nothing that is not put under him. But now we do not yet see all things put under him. **But we see Jesus**, who was made a little lower than the*

*angels, for the suffering of death **crowned** with **glory** and **honour**, that He, by the grace of God, might taste death for everyone.'*

Jesus had power over the following:

1. Power over creation

What was the first miracle Jesus ever did? He turned water into wine. He could also walk on water, calm the storm and feed 5,000 with only five small loaves and two small fishes and then tell His disciples to gather up the crumbs resulting in their gathering up twelve baskets full. Let's look at one of the scriptures, Matthew 8:26:

> *'But He said to them, "Why are you fearful, O you of little faith?" Then He arose and rebuked the winds and the sea, and there was a great calm.'*

Jesus had power over creation. Jesus did miracles with creation and gives us the power to perform miracles as well, but we very seldom see one.

In 1983 we ran a Youth Camp in the Transkei in South Africa. More children attended than those who had booked and this resulted in a shortage of food. The camp ended on Sunday evening and the seventeen of us who organized the camp stayed on until Monday morning as we had a 200-kilometre drive to the nearest town. Our host prayed over our breakfast and seeing only a small amount of cereal in the cereal box decided to give us a spoon each. She then began to spoon the cereal into the seventeen bowls and seeing there was still some left, carried on spooning and spooning and spooning until there were seventeen bowls full of cereal and still the same amount in the cereal box. Only then did we realize a miracle had happened. What a wonderful way to end a camp!

2. Power over demons and sickness

Jesus drove out demons wherever He went and healed all who came to Him. It is interesting that Jesus dealt with deliverance and sickness in a similar way. That is because both came from the devil. Matthew 8:16:

> 'When evening had come, they brought to Him many who were demon-possessed. And He cast out the spirits with a word, and healed all who were sick.'

Today Jesus will still drive out demons and heal the sick, that is, when He can find someone who believes Him and has the faith to walk in the area of deliverance and healing.

In Africa I have watched the Lord deliver many people. Once a hundred people came forward for deliverance and the Lord told me to treat it in the same way as for the sick. So I pointed and said, 'Every demonic spirit, every witchcraft spirit, every curse, every demonic thing, leave these people now in Jesus' name.' I stood back in amazement as eighty people were instantly set free; some screamed, others fell to the floor. After five minutes eighty people raised their hands having been delivered and went to sit down. I then prayed for the last twenty individually until all were set free. After that I prayed for the sick, telling them to put their own hand on their sickness or pain and receive their healing in Jesus' name. There were five blind people healed that morning plus many suffering from other sicknesses. Jesus is still healing the sick today and you can move into this area as well, for it is Jesus alone who does it.

3. Power to forgive sin
Matthew 9:2 says:

> 'Then behold, they brought to Him a paralytic lying on a bed. When Jesus saw their faith, He said to the paralytic, "Son, be of good cheer; your sins are forgiven you."'

4. Power to raise the dead
Jesus had the power to raise the dead and even waited four days before calling Lazarus forth as described in John 11:43:

'Now when He had said these things, He cried with a loud voice, "Lazarus, come forth!"'

Then Jesus did something even more incredible than that, for He Himself rose from the dead in three days in complete victory over sin and death and over every scheme of the devil.

Even today Jesus is still raising the dead and He can use anyone to do it. He does not always use the big men of God to do this either, but can choose anyone.

One of our team in Malawi, twenty-six years of age, not even a pastor, visits a hospital near Blantyre after church every Sunday to pray for the sick. On the 7th August 2005 he was not allowed into the front entrance of the hospital because of repair work, so he went round the back and entered through the mortuary. Seeing a young-looking dead man to his right, he felt the Lord wanted him to pray for the man. He went up to the man and said, 'In the name of Jesus sit up' and to his amazement, the dead man sat up alive and well.

The whole hospital praised the Lord that day and the doctors insisted he stayed in hospital for two days for observation. The man was thirty-six years old and had died of malaria. Now he was also completely healed so, after two days, he was allowed to go home.

So What Did Jesus' Dying on the Cross Result in for Us?

1. The breaking of the power of sin and death
Jesus' death on the cross became necessary, following the Fall, because God had made it clear that anyone who sinned, even once, would be cut off from Him forever, once they had physically died, and that no one could ever redeem themselves by any method whatsoever. The only cure would be the death of the sinless person who, in dying, took on Himself the punishment that would otherwise have to be paid by the sinner, i.e. us. God said, 'The soul who sins shall die' (Ezekiel 18:20). God sent His

Son, Jesus, who being fully God as well as fully man, was perfect, i.e. sinless, and therefore able to become the sacrifice and He died on our behalf, so taking our punishment. He died in our place. So long as we individually accept that we are sinners and separated from God and that He, Jesus, has died for each one of us personally, we can live in newness of life by accepting Jesus into our hearts.

The threefold purpose of water baptism is set out in Colossians 2:12 where the repentant sinner is:

> *'buried with Him in baptism, in which you also were raised with Him through faith in the working of God, who raised Him from the dead.'*

- *Death* – into the water. As we go into the water we are saying our old sinful nature is done away with. We are free from slavery to sin. There is a complete break with the past.
- *Burial* – under the water. Just as Jesus was buried in the tomb, so as we are baptised under the water our lives as sinners are put out of sight, as Paul explains in Romans 6:4:

> *'Therefore we were buried with Him through baptism into death, that just as Christ was raised from the dead by the glory of the Father, even so we also should walk in newness of life.'*

- *Resurrection* – out of the water. Romans 6:5 says:

> *'For if we have been united together in the likeness of His death, certainly we also shall be in the likeness of His resurrection.'*

Jesus was raised by the power of God. We are lifted out of the water to live a new life with Christ, as Galatians 2:20 says:

> *'I have been crucified with Christ; it is no longer I who live, but Christ lives in me; and the life which I now live in the flesh I*

live by faith in the Son of God, who loved me and gave Himself for me.'

In John 6:39 Jesus says:

'And this is the will of him who sent me, that I shall lose none of all that he has given me, but raise them up at the last day.'

Jesus has also given us eternal life.

2. Power to live in Christ's victory whilst still alive on this earth

In John 14:12–13, Jesus says:

'Most assuredly, I say to you, he who believes in Me, the works that I do he will do also; and greater works than these he will do, because I go to My Father. And whatever you ask in My name, that I will do, that the Father may be glorified in the Son.'

On the cross Jesus reversed what man had brought on himself in the Garden of Eden. Jesus Himself has made it possible for us to receive this glorious victory from Him, and the power of the Holy Spirit to live it.

So the next questions are:

- How do we receive this glorious victory?
- How do we receive this victory that Jesus has made available to us through the Holy Spirit?

After we have accepted Jesus into our heart as Lord and Saviour the baptism and giftings of the Holy Spirit are available to us. Then a wonderful change takes place.

It says in 1 John 4:4:

'You are of God, little children, and have overcome them, because He who is in you is greater than he who is in the world.'

The Holy Spirit within us is greater than the one who is in the world. The Holy Spirit connects us with our Father in Heaven in the heavenly realm, for it also goes on to say in John 3:34:

> *'For He whom God has sent speaks the words of God, for God does not give the Spirit by measure.'*

In other words, God gives the Spirit without limit.

When we spend time with God in the heavenly realm, He fills us and fills us and fills us with the Holy Spirit and then sends us forth to flow with rivers of living water. What glorious service: limitless power to heal the sick, gifts of the Spirit given without measure! These never run dry as long as we spend time in prayer receiving this glorious love, joy, peace, instruction, giftings and all we need to witness His power on earth, that man may be saved from the destruction of sin and death and live instead in righteousness to our Lord. We are also given power over sin. We are told in 1 Corinthians 10:13:

> *'No temptation has seized you except what is common to man. And God is faithful; he will not let you be tempted beyond what you can bear. But when you are tempted, he will also provide a way out so that you can stand up under it.'*   (NIV)

We therefore have no excuse, for we have all been given power over sin.

3. Authority and power over the enemy
Luke 10:19 tells us:

> *'I have given you authority to trample on snakes and scorpions and to overcome all the power of the enemy; nothing will harm you.'*   (NIV)

I need this verse in Africa so very much. This gives me boldness when I have to come against witch-doctors and all kinds of evil spirits.

In Cameroon we had to visit a seaside village built on volcanic rock from a nearby volcano. This village was under the curse of witch-doctors, marine spirits and the occult. Even the elders of the village were involved and two had been arrested for horrible crimes.

We were supposed to have been somewhere else, but the pastor never showed up to collect us, and we had not gone to Cameroon to sit doing nothing, so the pastor in Nimba phoned Pastor Emmanuel, and Emmanuel said, *'Please come. These are the white people we have been waiting for to set our village free.'* Pastor Emmanuel had had a vision on the sixth of that month, that white people from Europe would come and set the village free from witchcraft, and had told the whole village of this. So two hours later, we arrived and bound the evil spirits to whom the residents had given their hearts, and commanded, in the spirit realm, that the hearts be given back to the people for the duration of the services for three days, so that the people could make a choice between the evil spirits and Christ.

The pastor then went round the village with a hand megaphone telling everyone that the white people he had prophesied about on the sixth of that month were here and invited everyone to come to this meeting. Soon the church was full. I preached a strong gospel message and about fifty came forward to receive Christ, then about twenty people were delivered from evil spirits and about fifty received their healing.

At the end another lady came forward complaining that a certain person had put witchcraft curses on her. We cut her off from the curses and asked her to forgive this person, and to give this lady the gospel. She said she would do this.

Suddenly Rev. Henry Coles, who came with us, prophesied that if a certain lady, who kept putting curses on God's people, did not repent of this wickedness after she had been given the gospel message, she would die within three days. I was rather perturbed that Henry should give such a negative prophecy in front of the whole church.

The next day we were invited back to an overflowing church and even had to pray for those outside. By now, over a hundred people had received Christ and about the same number had received healing and testified, giving glory to God. There were also about sixty who had received deliverance.

The next day, Saturday, Pastor Emmanuel came running to tell us that the person who had put so many curses upon the lady whom the Lord delivered, had been told the gospel, but instead of receiving Christ, had gone straight back to the witch-doctor to deliver more curses on this lady; but the powers of witchcraft were not working. So, she had to go to another village to put a curse on this lady. As she was returning from this village with the curse she dropped dead. This had a very positive effect on the village, which not only had seen the love and healing power of Christ, but also the death through the sins of those who prefer to practise evil. We are not fighting against flesh and blood, but against the principalities of evil. Through this lady's death many more received Jesus as Lord and Saviour.

This was a God-ordained visit and we certainly saw the power of God at work over every demonic force. I also saw Luke 10:19 in a new light, and also Romans 8:37 which says:

> *'Yet in all these things we are more than conquerors through Him who loved us.'*

Philippians 4:13 encourages us by saying:

> *'I can do all things through Christ who strengthens me.'*

We can walk in the power of His strength and we also have authority to conquer sin, sickness, and all the power of the enemy in Jesus' name.

How do we further exercise this power and victory over Satan?

Ephesians 6:13–17 says:

> 'Therefore take up the whole armour of God, that you may be able to withstand in the evil day, and having done all, to stand. Stand therefore, having girded your waist with truth, having put on the breastplate of righteousness, and having shod your feet with the preparation of the gospel of peace; above all, taking the shield of faith with which you will be able to quench all the fiery darts of the wicked one. And take the helmet of salvation, and the sword of the Spirit, which is the word of God.'

Be self-controlled, as we are instructed in 1 Peter 5:8:

> 'Be sober, be vigilant; because your adversary the devil walks about like a roaring lion, seeking whom he may devour.'

We must be alert in order that Satan might not outwit us, for 'we are not unaware of his schemes' (2 Corinthians 2:11, NIV).

We have to resist temptation. James 1:13 helps us specifically by saying:

> 'Let no one say when he is tempted, "I am tempted by God"; for God cannot be tempted by evil, nor does He Himself tempt anyone.'

We need wisdom to discern Satan's deceiving methods. 2 Corinthians 11:14 cautions:

> 'And no wonder! For Satan himself transforms himself into an angel of light.'

We need to test all by the Word of God:

> 'But we have renounced the hidden things of shame, not walking in craftiness nor handling the word of God deceitfully, but by

manifestation of the truth commending ourselves to every man's
conscience in the sight of God.'   (2 Corinthians 4:2)

If we do these things we will have full victory over the devil.
Revelation 12:10 encourages us with these words:

'And I heard a loud voice in heaven, saying, "Now the salvation
and the power and the kingdom of our God and the authority of
his Christ have come, for the accuser of our brothers has been
thrown down, who accuses them day and night before our God." '
                                                              (ESV)

How Should We Then Live?

In Matthew 5:13 Jesus informs us:

'You are the salt of the earth; but if the salt loses its flavour, how
shall it be seasoned? It is then good for nothing but to be thrown
out and trampled underfoot by men.'

We must be the salt of the earth. In Matthew 5:14 Jesus adds:

'You are the light of the world. A city that is set on a hill cannot be
hidden.'

We must be the light to the world. 1 Corinthians 6:17 declares:

'But he who is joined to the Lord is one spirit with Him.'

We must unite ourselves with the Lord in prayer so that, as it
says in John 14:20:

'At that day you will know that I am in My Father, and you in
Me, and I in you.'

This is the most wonderful thing we can ever know and then we are further encouraged through the words found in 2 Corinthians 5:17:

> *'Therefore, if anyone is in Christ, he is a new creation; old things have passed away; behold, all things have become new.'*

We become new creations in Christ. Not only that, we become members of His body. Ephesians 5:30 says:

> *'For we are members of His body, of His flesh and of His bones.'*

We become members of Jesus' Body – flesh, bones and Spirit. If we are therefore members of the Body of Christ we also share His victory over evil. This is reflected in Jesus' words of Luke 10:19:

> *'Behold, I give you the authority to trample on serpents and scorpions, and over all the power of the enemy, and nothing shall by any means hurt you.'*

We share in Christ's power and authority over the enemy. Ephesians 6:13 commands us:

> *'Therefore take up the whole armour of God, that you may be able to withstand in the evil day, and having done all, to stand.'*

We have Christ's finest armour; invisible yet empowered with His strength. James 4:7 tells us:

> *'Therefore submit to God. Resist the devil and he will flee from you.'*

We can reign in life now with Jesus by submitting to God, not from duty but willingly and happily. The very next verse, James 4:8, offers further encouragement:

> *'Draw near to God and He will draw near to you. Cleanse your hands, you sinners; and purify your hearts, you double-minded.'*

We can live very near to God. Ephesians 6:10 goes even further:

> *'Finally, my brethren, be strong in the Lord and in the power of His might.'*

We have His strength and mighty power available to us. Matthew 5:13 exhorts us to be the salt of the earth and Matthew 5:15 exhorts us to be light to the world.

And what does God give us all this for?

2 Timothy 2:1–2 persuades us thus:

> *'You therefore, my son, be strong in the grace that is in Christ Jesus. And the things that you have heard from me among many witnesses, commit these to faithful men who will be able to teach others also.'*

Mark 16:15–18 reminds us of the great commission:

> *'And He said to them, "Go into all the world and preach the gospel to every creature. He who believes and is baptized will be saved; but he who does not believe will be condemned. And these signs will follow those who believe: In My name they will cast out demons; they will speak with new tongues; they will take up serpents; and if they drink anything deadly, it will by no means hurt them; they will lay hands on the sick, and they will recover." '*

We must present the Word of God to all men, cast out demons, heal the sick and the gates of Hell will not prevail against us.

Some Questions to Think About

- What was the result of Adam and Eve eating the fruit of the Tree of the Knowledge of Good and Evil?
- Why does the devil go to so much effort to cause man to sin, inflict sickness, curses, lies etc.?
- What did God do about it?
- What did Jesus' dying on the cross achieve for us?
- How should we then live?
- Would you like to be baptised in the Holy Spirit? Then pray this:

  Lord Jesus, thank You that it is Your will that I be baptised in the Holy Spirit. I turn from any sin and want to live for You in every way. Please Lord baptise me in the Holy Spirit. Thank You, Jesus. Amen.

Many receive healing and respond to Jesus,
accepting Him as Lord and Saviour

The Kingdom of God Is at Hand

In 1 Chronicles 29:11–13 King David prayed:

> 'Yours, O LORD, is the greatness,
> The power and the glory,
> The victory and the majesty;
> For all that is in heaven and in earth is Yours;
> Yours is the kingdom, O LORD,
> And You are exalted as head over all.
> Both riches and honour come from You,
> And You reign over all.
> In Your hand is power and might;
> In Your hand it is to make great
> And to give strength to all.
> Now therefore, our God,
> We thank You
> And praise Your glorious name.'

What is this scripture actually saying to us? Psalm 145:10–13 says:

> 'All Your works shall praise You, O LORD,
> And Your saints shall bless You.
> They shall speak of the glory of Your kingdom,
> And talk of Your power,

> *To make known to the sons of men His mighty acts,*
> *And the glorious majesty of His kingdom.*
> *Your kingdom is an everlasting kingdom,*
> *And Your dominion endures throughout all generations.'*

The Old Testament is looking forward to something wonderful happening. We read in Isaiah 9:6–7:

> *'For unto us a Child is born,*
> *Unto us a Son is given;*
> *And the government will be upon His shoulder.*
> *And His name will be called*
> *Wonderful, Counsellor, Mighty God,*
> *Everlasting Father, Prince of Peace.*
> *Of the increase of His government and peace*
> *There will be no end,*
> *Upon the throne of David and over His kingdom,*
> *To order it and establish it with judgment and justice*
> *From that time forward, even forever.*
> *The zeal of the* LORD *of hosts will perform this.'*

In Luke 1:32–33 the angel Gabriel confirms how Jesus fulfils Isaiah 9:

> *'He will be great, and will be called the Son of the Highest; and*
> *the Lord God will give Him the throne of His father David. And*
> *He will reign over the house of Jacob forever, and of His kingdom*
> *there will be no end.'*

Jesus has already come!! His Kingdom has already come. The Kingdom of God is already at hand, and the Old Testament prophesies it. Daniel 4:2–3 says:

> *'I thought it good to declare the signs and wonders that the*
> *Most High God has worked for me.*

> *How great are His signs,*
> *And how mighty His wonders!*
> *His kingdom is an everlasting kingdom,*
> *And His dominion is from generation to generation.'*

Here Daniel speaks of signs and wonders of his everlasting kingdom being performed from generation to generation. Daniel continues in 7:27 to say:

> *'Then the kingdom and dominion,*
> *And the greatness of the kingdoms under the whole heaven,*
> *Shall be given to the people, the saints of the Most High.*
> *His kingdom is an everlasting kingdom,*
> *And all dominions shall serve and obey Him.'*

Here the Old Testament speaks of signs and wonders being given to God's saints. That is us!! Jesus gave this through the cross. The New International Version Bible notes say; *'handed over to the saints for their benefit. God and the Messiah will rule'* – is this for when Jesus comes again at His second coming, or is it also for the time between the first coming and the second coming? Let's see what the New Testament says. Matthew 3:1–2 tells us:

> *'In those days John the Baptist came preaching in the wilderness of Judea, and saying, "Repent, for the kingdom of heaven is at hand!"'*

Other translations replace *'is at hand'* with *'is near'*. In Matthew 3:3 John the Baptist continues:

> *'For this is he who was spoken of by the prophet Isaiah, saying:*
>
> > *"The voice of one crying in the wilderness:*
> > *'Prepare the way of the LORD;*
> > *Make His paths straight.'"'*

The NIV study notes says *'Repent – make a radical change in one's life.'* The 'Kingdom of Heaven' is found in Matthew thirty-three times. The Kingdom of Heaven is the rule of God and is both a present reality and a future hope. The idea of God's Kingdom is central to Jesus' teaching and is mentioned fifty times in Matthew alone. This says that the Kingdom of God has been given to us after the first coming of Jesus as well as after the second coming of Jesus. It is available to all who believe.

In Matthew 4:16–17 we have a great statement, summarizing Isaiah 9:

> *' "The people who sat in darkness have seen a great light,*
> *And upon those who sat in the region and shadow of death*
> *Light has dawned."*
>
> *From that time Jesus began to preach and to say, "Repent, for the kingdom of heaven is at hand." '*

Jesus began His public ministry with the same message as John the Baptist – repent because God's reign was drawing near in the person and ministry of Jesus. In Matthew 4:23 we read:

> *'And Jesus went about all Galilee, teaching in their synagogues, preaching the gospel of the kingdom, and healing all kinds of sickness and all kinds of disease among the people.'*

Jesus showed us in these signs that the Kingdom of God was at hand and tells us to seek the Kingdom as well. Matthew 6:33 Jesus similarly promises:

> *'But seek first the kingdom of God and His righteousness, and all these things shall be added to you.'*

When we seek His Kingdom, we are seeking the higher Kingdom, for the Kingdom of Heaven, or of God, is higher and greater than this worldly kingdom.

Matthew 10:1 informs us that Jesus instructed His disciples thus:

> 'And when He had called His twelve disciples to Him, He gave them power over unclean spirits, to cast them out, and to heal all kinds of sickness and all kinds of disease.'

Similarly in Matthew 10:6–7 we read how Jesus commands them:

> 'But go rather to the lost sheep of the house of Israel. And as you go, preach, saying, "The kingdom of heaven is at hand."'

So He gave them authority to preach that the Kingdom of Heaven is at hand and then to demonstrate that it was at hand by healing every disease and every infirmity.

Now the Pharisees asked Jesus when the Kingdom was coming. In Luke 17:20–21 we read Jesus' response:

> 'Now when He was asked by the Pharisees when the kingdom of God would come, He answered them and said, "The kingdom of God does not come with observation; nor will they say, 'See here!' or 'See there!' For indeed, the kingdom of God is within you."'

Jesus is the Kingdom of God and He was in their midst. But if Jesus dwells in our hearts, then He too, is in the midst of us.

The Kingdom of God is in the spiritual realm, brought upon us by the Holy Spirit. We can receive Him now. We can walk in this spiritual realm now. We can receive the power and authority of Jesus' name now and, as we preach, the Kingdom of God is at hand with the gospel. Jesus will do it. Signs and wonders will follow our preaching, for the Kingdom of God has come.

But then, why are we not all walking it? There are some reasons for this. John 3:5 says:

> '*Jesus answered, "Most assuredly, I say to you, unless one is born of water and the Spirit, he cannot enter the kingdom of God."* '

We must be born of the Holy Spirit. Romans 14:17 says:

> '...*for the kingdom of God is not eating and drinking, but righteousness and peace and joy in the Holy Spirit.*'

Pray, seeking to be filled with God's righteousness and peace and joy and to be filled daily with the Holy Spirit. Acts 14:22 records that Paul and Barnabas returned to Lystra:

> '...*strengthening the souls of the disciples, exhorting them to continue in the faith, and saying, "We must through many tribulations enter the kingdom of God."* '

We must allow God to test us, sift us, and change us, to work out our salvation in dying to self and allowing Him complete reign over us. We have to count the cost and do it. For what we give up will never compare with what He can do in and through us.

1 Corinthians 15:50 advises:

> '*Now this I say, brethren, that flesh and blood cannot inherit the kingdom of God; nor does corruption inherit incorruption.*'

The Lord has to sift us first of the desires of the flesh, then He can pour His power through us. We learn in 1 Corinthians 4:20:

> '*For the kingdom of God does not consist in talk but in power.*'
>
> (ESV)

This is the demonstration of the power that the Lord gives to us when we receive the Holy Spirit. As the resurrected Jesus says in Acts 1:8:

> *'But you shall receive power when the Holy Spirit has come upon you; and you shall be witnesses to Me in Jerusalem, and in all Judea and Samaria, and to the end of the earth.'*

This demonstration of the power of the Holy Spirit is given to us that we may become His witnesses to the power of the cross to all men near and far.

Romans 1:16 tells us Paul's declaration:

> *'For I am not ashamed of the gospel of Christ, for it is the power of God to salvation for everyone who believes, for the Jew first and also for the Greek.'*

This power is given to us so that we may preach the gospel of salvation in order that souls may be saved. 1 Corinthians 2:4–5 further demonstrates Paul's commitment:

> *'And my speech and my preaching were not with persuasive words of human wisdom, but in demonstration of the Spirit and of power, that your faith should not be in the wisdom of men but in the power of God.'*

We are to preach the gospel with the demonstration of His power. 1 Thessalonians 1:5 states:

> *'For our gospel did not come to you in word only, but also in power, and in the Holy Spirit and in much assurance, as you know what kind of men we were among you for your sake.'*

When we receive the gospel in this way, we receive the glorious salvation with both word and power. We have seen with our own eyes and heart that Jesus Christ is Lord. 2 Peter 1:3 reminds us,

> *'His divine power has given to us all things that pertain to life and godliness, through the knowledge of Him who called us by glory and virtue.'*

I believe this is only possible because the Kingdom of God is at hand right now in our midst. It is up to us to receive it.

How do we receive it?

It is by getting to know our Father in Heaven, by spending time with Him in regular prayer. By listening to Him to show us, to teach us, speak to us, open the Scriptures to us, to fill us with His gifts and to fill us with His power and authority of His Holy Spirit to do His work here on earth. Acts 4:33 says:

> '*And with great power the apostles gave witness to the resurrection of the Lord Jesus. And great grace was upon them all.*'

Was all this great power and demonstration of the Holy Spirit in saving, healing and delivering people from evil to just stop with the apostles or was it for us as well?

Acts 6:8 tells of Stephen's activity:

> '*And Stephen, full of faith and power, did great wonders and signs among the people.*'

Here we see that Stephen, who was not one of the twelve apostles, was also witnessing in the power and demonstration of the Holy Spirit. Then in Romans 15:13 it says:

> '*May the God of hope fill you with all joy and peace as you trust in him, so that you may overflow with hope by the power of the Holy Spirit.*' (NIV)

Paul is speaking to us, the Church, so that in believing we are filled with joy and peace, secure in God's love, so that His power in the Holy Spirit may operate through us in power to do three things.

Mark 6:12–13 tells us that the twelve disciples:

> '. . . *went out and preached that people should repent. And they cast out many demons, and anointed with oil many who were sick, and healed them.*'

So Jesus sent out the twelve to teach salvation, deliverance and healing. Then He sent the seventy out to do the same, and then Stephen and Philip and all the great men of God down through modern history right up to this very day. We read about some of the results from Philip's witness to the gospel.

Acts 8:6–8 says:

> *'And the multitudes with one accord heeded the things spoken by Philip, hearing and seeing the miracles which he did. For unclean spirits, crying with a loud voice, came out of many who were possessed; and many who were paralysed and lame were healed. And there was great joy in that city.'*

How can it be that these people also flowed in this authority and power of the Holy Spirit?

In Colossians 2:14–15 we read:

> *'... having cancelled the written code, with its regulations, that was against us and that stood opposed to us; he took it away, nailing it to the cross. And having disarmed the powers and authorities, he made a public spectacle of them, triumphing over them by the cross.'* (NIV)

Jesus' death and resurrection cancelled the written code of the Old Testament Law as the basis of our righteousness. Jesus cancelled it on the cross and enabled the Kingdom of Heaven to be at hand for each one of us, when we believe it, when we receive it, when we live it.

John 14:12–13 declares:

> *'I tell you the truth, anyone who has faith in me will do what I have been doing. He will do even greater things than these, because I am going to the Father. And I will do whatever you ask in my name, so that the Son may bring glory to the Father.'* (NIV)

By going to the Father Jesus has enabled His Kingdom of Heaven to be at hand. It is done! Jesus has done it on the cross. The cross has brought the Kingdom of God to each one of us, who will receive Him, and live in Him.

Some Questions to Think About

- What is the Old Testament looking forward to?
- What did John the Baptist preach?
- What did Jesus demonstrate to us?
- Is the Kingdom of God at hand for us today?
- Jesus' death and resurrection cancelled the effects of sin and death. What does this mean for us?

The Gift of Righteousness

What is righteousness? It means a person who is right, wise, just, upright, good, true, proper, correct, real, genuine, exact, satisfactory, suitable, well, someone who releases from injustice. A wise person will want to be right, will want to be righteous. Righteousness produces authority. Authority produces power and power effects great change. Let's look at James 5:16–18:

> *'Confess your trespasses to one another, and pray for one another, that you may be healed. The effective, fervent prayer of a righteous man avails much. Elijah was a man with a nature like ours, and he prayed earnestly that it would not rain; and it did not rain on the land for three years and six months. And he prayed again, and the heaven gave rain, and the earth produced its fruit.'*

The prayer of a righteous man has great power in its effects. Elijah was a man of like nature to us. He prayed fervently that it would not rain: and for three years and six months it did not rain on the earth. Then he prayed again and the heavens gave rain, and the earth brought forth its fruit.

Jesus had perfect righteousness; He knew no sin. He had authority over all creation and all evil. He turned water into wine, walked on water, calmed the storms and fed 5,000 people with five loaves and two fishes. He had authority to forgive sin.

He had authority to cast out demons. He had authority to cast out sickness and heal the sick. He even had power to raise the dead. He waited four days before He called Lazarus to come forth from his tomb. Jesus then went on to the cross, was crucified, and died. On the third day He rose in complete and total victory in triumph over every sin, sickness and every demonic thing. He then ascended to the Father where He sits today at His right hand above every rule and authority, power and dominion and above every name that is named. Jesus says in John 14:12:

> 'Most assuredly, I say to you, he who believes in Me, the works that I do he will do also; and greater works than these he will do, because I go to My Father.'

But where do we see anyone doing what Jesus did? Why not? Who is walking in the anointing, authority and power of the Holy Spirit to do God's work without hindrance? We all ask the Lord for a stronger anointing. How are we limiting the anointing that the Lord wants to pour through us? How can we serve the Lord to our fullest calling and potential?

The Lord sometimes speaks to us in the strangest places, probably where He can get our attention best. I was on the London Underground on my way to speak at a church, when the Lord revealed to me something fantastic. As I got off at my destination I just had to stop and write, as hundreds of people went their way. I suddenly realized that the devil has no regard for his own, no respect for them whatever. Let's read Acts 19:15–16:

> 'And the evil spirit answered and said, "Jesus I know, and Paul I know; but who are you?" Then the man in whom the evil spirit was leaped on them, overpowered them, and prevailed against them, so that they fled out of that house naked and wounded.'

The devil has no respect for a sinner. A sinner the devil can control. If the devil can tempt a man to sin and that man sins, then the devil has authority and power over that man, but he whom the devil does not succeed in causing to sin, he has no power over. In the wilderness the devil tempted Jesus but Jesus would not give in to the temptation. Instead Jesus answered the devil with the Word of God in Scripture and remained sinless. Jesus was not going to give His authority and power to the devil, never. When we pursue righteousness something glorious happens to us. Walking in Christ's righteousness gives us authority and power over the devil, over demons and sickness and every demonic power. Nothing can harm us. We read in Luke 10:17–20 of how the disciples returned to Jesus after going on mission for Him:

> *'Then the seventy returned with joy, saying, "Lord, even the demons are subject to us in Your name." And He said to them, "I saw Satan fall like lightning from heaven. Behold, I give you the authority to trample on serpents and scorpions, and over all the power of the enemy, and nothing shall by any means hurt you. Nevertheless do not rejoice in this, that the spirits are subject to you, but rather rejoice because your names are written in heaven." '*

Does this mean that the more we pursue righteousness and become more righteous in Jesus, the more authority and power we will have over the enemy, and we will see the greater miracles happen?

I believe that we need to have less and less sin within us to hinder God's miraculous power from moving through us to the ones He loves so much and wants to heal and set free. God's ways are different from the world's ways.

God's ways	The world's way
Love convicts of sin	Rules condemn sin
Love encourages righteousness	Sin entices the flesh
The Spirit man looks to God	The fleshly man gratifies self
The cross gives freedom from sin	The world uses human authority to control man

Righteousness gives authority over sin

Power effects changed lives

The world rules man with the law

Worldly power controls man

How does God deal with sin?

God's love searches out the lost and hurt

God sent His only Son to die on the cross to set man free

God forgives those who repent

God gives the Bible to correct sin and encourage

A man who accepts Christ learns righteousness, for his heart is changed

A man convicted of sin will turn from it and grow into Christ in righteousness

How does the world deal with sin?

Sin abounds in every form in enticing ways

Man makes laws to control sin

Man puts sinners into prison

A prison sentence hopefully corrects man

A man in jail may or may not learn righteousness for his heart is unchanged

A convicted man with no heart change may do the same evil again

With God

God deals with man through grace

Forgiveness of sin gives freedom

Freedom from sin gives authority over sin

Authority over sin gives power to live in righteousness

Living in righteousness effects great change in and through one's life and gives eternal life

Righteousness is light and freedom

Without God

The world deals with man through the law

Jailing the sinner controls the sin

Sin condemns us, sin controls man

Sin has power to destroy man

The sinner will die in his sin and spend eternity without Christ in Hell

Sin is darkness and bondage

This is why it is so important to reach out to the people in our world with the saving grace of Jesus.

Some time ago, my horse, George, was stolen complete with saddle and bridle, by a very unreasonable lady. (She believed that having a partially disabled daughter, who had fallen in love with him, entitled her to take the horse whilst I was away in Africa.)

I knew I would not get far with her by using the police and the law. I went to the Lord. He led me to Matthew 5:40,

> 'And if someone wants to sue you and take your tunic, let him have your cloak also.'

'Lord, how will that scripture get George back?'

'Wait', came the reply.

So I waited and did nothing for three months. One day the Lord said to me, 'Today, put two hundred pounds in ten pound notes in an envelope. Get into your horsebox and drive over to where you horse is and the lady will release your horse to you.' I instantly obeyed and drove over to the stables in anticipation of what would happen.

I arrived. The lady, daughter and George were there. I prayed and I approached the lady and sat on a straw bale beside her. 'I know that you are really a good lady,' I said. 'And I know you are going to do the right thing concerning George so I have brought you this gift as I know that you are going to release George to me today so that I can take him home with me this morning.'

She took the envelope and counted the money slowly and looked up and said, 'Yes, I will release your horse to you. You can take him with you now.'

The excitement surged as I took my horse who seemed to sense he was coming home and eagerly walked straight up the ramp into the horsebox.

Next day the phone rang. The lady who had stolen George said, 'Suzanne, I need to ask you a question that really has been puzzling me. I stole George from you, I did wrong and you, you did nothing for three months and then after all that you come and give me a gift of money. How could you do that to someone who has stolen your best horse?'

I replied, 'Because Jesus loves you and Jesus loves your daughter so much, He told me to do it that way.'

'Jesus loves *me*? You mean to say Jesus loves me after all the wrong I have done?'

'Yes, Jesus loves you so much that He died on the cross, so that if you will turn from sin, believe in Him, He will forgive you and give you eternal life.'

'I want to turn from sin right now,' she blurted out. 'I want to believe in Jesus right now. I promise you I will never hurt you or anyone else again. Please will you pray for me.'

I prayed with her and led her to Jesus, and now I can trust her.

The love of God and His righteousness overcomes every sin, every barrier. His love turns the heart of stone into a heart of flesh.

This experience really taught me how much God is in control of every single thing when we trust Him and obey Him. During those three months the Lord caused George to refuse to jump anything for the lady's daughter, so she did not like the horse so much any more. She could release him more easily; yet as soon as George came home he jumped all the jumps normally. This also showed me that the Lord cared enough for me to bring my horse back to me, so I no longer had to take out horseback riders whilst on foot myself.

God's ways of doing things are very different from the world's way of doing things. It does take time to learn God's ways and then to do things His way – His ways always work.

In all the problems that life may throw your way, Jesus was faced with a type of them too. If you go to the Gospels with your situation and find out where Jesus faced a similar problem and you then handle that problem in a similar way to the way Jesus did, then you will be guaranteed the same success as Jesus was. This is now the way that I go through life and handle things. I simply do it '*Jesus' way*'.

Jesus' way of doing things is always the righteous way, the way of love and forgiveness. This is the way that causes sinners to repent and be reconciled to God. In fact righteousness is a gift that is more precious than a diamond – spotless, transparent, reflecting light in every direction, flawless, extravagant, shining forth its beauty to all.

It takes much work to cut a diamond. Every flaw must be removed. Nothing must mar its beauty, and nothing must limit its reflection. A diamond is a gift of flawless beauty; the transparency brings life to light in its reflection of it. So God works in our lives to fashion and perfect us into all righteousness that we may become a true transparent reflection of His glorious light and love and purity. It is then that we become as a diamond in His hands as we are reminded in 2 Corinthians 3:18:

> *'But we all, with unveiled face, beholding as in a mirror the glory of the Lord, are being transformed into the same image from glory to glory, just as by the Spirit of the Lord.'*

How can we be changed into His likeness from one degree of glory into another? 1 Corinthians 1:30 advises us:

> *'But of Him you are in Christ Jesus, who became for us wisdom from God – and righteousness and sanctification and redemption.'*

'To sanctify' is to make holy and set apart for God. 'Redemption' rescues and delivers us from evil. Proverbs 2:9 says:

> *'Then you will understand righteousness and justice, Equity and every good path.'*

Psalm 112:1 says:

> *'Praise the LORD! Blessed is the man who fears the LORD, Who delights greatly in His commandments.'*

To 'fear the Lord' is wisdom and 'to shun all evil' is understanding. This means to fear to hurt God by any sin or unrighteousness and to seek His righteousness instead. Proverbs 21:21 advises:

*'He who follows righteousness and mercy
Finds life, righteousness and honour.'*

2 Corinthians 5:21 tells us:

*'For He made Him who knew no sin to be sin for us, that we
might become the righteousness of God in Him.'*

How can we become the righteousness of God? Romans 5:18–19
gives us an insight into this:

*'Therefore, as through one man's offence judgment came to all
men, resulting in condemnation, even so through one Man's
righteous act the free gift came to all men, resulting in justification
of life. For as by one man's disobedience many were made sinners,
so also by one Man's obedience many will be made righteous.'*

Jesus made this possible on the cross by dying in our place, to
give man a second chance to obey after what Adam and Eve had
brought upon mankind by eating of the fruit of the tree of
knowledge of good and evil. The gift of salvation is the saving
of people from the effect of evil and wrongdoing. The gift of
righteousness is freedom from wrongdoing and the doing
of right things like kindness, truthfulness, justice and care for
others. We have all been taught to turn from evil as it is written
in the following verses:

*'Treasures of wickedness profit nothing,
But righteousness delivers from death.'*   (Proverbs 10:2)

*'As righteousness leads to life,
So he who pursues evil pursues it to his own death.'*
(Proverbs 11:19)

*'In the way of righteousness is life,
And in its pathway there is no death.'*   (Proverbs 12:28)

We need to turn our backs on all evil and pursue God and His righteousness every moment of our lives. As we yield to God's ways and guidance we will come under His protection and be made more and more righteous. As we are reminded in 2 Timothy 3:16:

> *'All Scripture is given by inspiration of God, and is profitable for doctrine, for reproof, for correction, for instruction in righteousness.'*

And again in 1 Timothy 6:11:

> *'But you, O man of God, flee these things and pursue right-eousness, godliness, faith, love, patience, gentleness.'*

How do we actively pursue righteousness?

What happens when we do something wrong? We will come out of the presence of God and guilt will take hold of us. This can cause many reactions. Some may confess their sin, and others may try to excuse their sin. Note that in Philippians 3:9 Paul emphasised:

> *'. . . not having my own righteousness, which is from the law, but that which is through faith in Christ, the righteousness which is from God by faith.'*

What is this scripture saying? What does a child do when he does something wrong? Does he plead for forgiveness over and over? Is he afraid he will be thrown out of the house? No, he runs crying into his parents' arms where his parents will comfort and warn him of the dangers of what he has done and hopefully the child will never do that thing again, but has learned a lesson in righteousness and will walk in the area of righteousness. God treats us in the same way, though the consequence of that sin we still have to bear, even though we are forgiven.

Romans 4:3–8 speaks into the situation thus:

> *'For what does the Scripture say? "Abraham believed God, and it
> was accounted to him for righteousness." Now to him who works,
> the wages are not counted as grace but as debt. But to him who
> does not work but believes on Him who justifies the ungodly, his
> faith is accounted for righteousness, just as David also describes
> the blessedness of the man to whom God imputes righteousness
> apart from works:*
>
> > *"Blessed are those whose lawless deeds are forgiven,*
> > *And whose sins are covered;*
> > *Blessed is the man to whom the* LORD *shall not impute sin." ' '*

The reason for this is what the Lord has made available to us
through Jesus, as it says in Romans 3:21–26:

> *'But now the righteousness of God apart from the law is revealed,
> being witnessed by the Law and the Prophets, even the right-
> eousness of God, through faith in Jesus Christ, to all and on all
> who believe. For there is no difference; for all have sinned and fall
> short of the glory of God, being justified freely by His grace
> through the redemption that is in Christ Jesus, whom God set
> forth as a propitiation by His blood, through faith, to demonstrate
> His righteousness, because in His forbearance God had passed
> over the sins that were previously committed, to demonstrate at
> the present time His righteousness, that He might be just and the
> justifier of the one who has faith in Jesus.'*

This is glorious news for us. Salvation and righteousness are
linked together and both are received by faith. Further encouragement comes from Romans 1:17:

> *'For in the gospel a righteousness from God is revealed, a
> righteousness that is by faith from first to last, just as it is
> written: "The righteous will live by faith." '*   (NIV)

How should we then live? Romans 6:19 cautions us:

> *'I speak in human terms because of the weakness of your flesh. For just as you presented your members as slaves of uncleanness, and of lawlessness leading to more lawlessness, so now present your members as slaves of righteousness for holiness.'*

As we yield ourselves to the holiness of the Lord day by day by coming into His presence daily in prayer, He will enable us to become more and more righteous. Paul in Ephesians 4:24 exhorts:

> *'. . . that you put on the new man which was created according to God, in true righteousness and holiness.'*

When we spend time with God daily in prayer, we will take on His nature, just as we would by spending time with any person whom we admire.

Daniel 4:27 teaches us through words addressed to a king:

> *'Therefore, O king, let my advice be acceptable to you; break off your sins by being righteous, and your iniquities by showing mercy to the poor. Perhaps there may be a lengthening of your prosperity.'*

What will be the result of living in righteousness? The answer can be provided through three passages of Scripture:

> *'I put on righteousness, and it clothed me;*
> *My justice was like a robe and a turban.*
> *I was eyes to the blind,*
> *And I was feet to the lame.*
> *I was a father to the poor,*
> *And I searched out the case that I did not know.'*
>
> (Job 29:14–16)

> '*In righteousness you shall be established;*
> *You shall be far from oppression, for you shall not fear;*
> *And from terror, for it shall not come near you.*'
>
> (Isaiah 54:14)

> '*I will greatly rejoice in the* LORD,
> *My soul shall be joyful in my God;*
> *For He has clothed me with the garments of salvation,*
> *He has covered me with the robe of righteousness,*
> *As a bridegroom decks himself with ornaments,*
> *And as a bride adorns herself with her jewels.*'
>
> (Isaiah 61:10)

Righteousness changes us. Righteousness frees us. Righteousness brings us closer to Jesus, and then we come to see life as He sees life. We come to think as He would think. We come to love others as He loves others. Suddenly our priorities change. We no longer think of ourselves for we are happy and content in Christ. Now we see others before ourselves and want to go out in Jesus' name to preach, bring salvation, healing, deliverance and help to others who are dying in the clutches of evil. The following passages provide further help and insight:

> '*Your mercy, O* LORD, *is in the heavens;*
> *Your faithfulness reaches to the clouds.*
> *Your righteousness is like the great mountains;*
> *Your judgments are a great deep;*
> *O* LORD, *You preserve man and beast.*'   (Psalm 36:5–6)

> '*Let the heavens declare His righteousness,*
> *For God Himself is Judge*'   (Psalm 50:6)

> '*Also Your righteousness, O God, is very high,*
> *You who have done great things;*
> *O God, who is like You?*'   (Psalm 71:19)

> *'But let justice run down like water,*
> *And righteousness like a mighty stream.'* (Amos 5:24)

We don't just receive the gift of righteousness, we have to walk in it and live in it. A child cannot learn to walk unless he puts one leg in front of the other.

As we live in righteousness daily, pursuing it with all our hearts, so we become a treasure to our Lord and the Lord receives us as His treasure and gives to us the treasures of His love, joy, peace and also the Holy Spirit, to help us in the works He gives us to do. We see this in Exodus 19:5:

> *'Now therefore, if you will indeed obey My voice and keep My covenant, then you shall be a special treasure to Me above all people; for all the earth is Mine.'*

We become His ambassadors to the nations in whatever giftings God gives us. The more we live in righteousness, the greater God's power and authority will be manifested through our mere human frames and we will know the truth of 2 Corinthians 4:7:

> *'But we have this treasure in earthen vessels, that the excellence of the power may be of God and not of us.'*

Let us aim to live in the righteousness of God.

True Freedom

The gift of salvation and the gift of righteousness are the two greatest gifts in the universe, for it is these two gifts that bring us into true freedom in Christ.

> *'Then Jesus said to the Jews who believed in Him, "If you abide in My word, you are My disciples indeed. And you shall know the truth, and the truth shall set you free."*

> They answered Him, "We are Abraham's descendants, and
> have never been in bondage to anyone. How can you say, 'You
> will be made free?'"
>
> Jesus answered them, "Most assuredly, I say to you, whoever
> commits sin is a slave to sin. And a slave does not abide in the
> house forever, but a son abides forever. Therefore if the Son makes
> you free, you shall be free indeed."'   (John 8:31–36)

Everyone who commits sin is a slave to sin. This is not talking
about political freedom or even freedom from prison bars, it is
something much deeper, something from within.

In the Philippines I visited the prison. 'Why are you here?'
I asked.

'I did this or that wrong [i.e. I sinned].'

'Why did you do it?'

'I don't know. I just did it.'

'Did you want to do it?'

'No.'

'Then, why did you do it?'

'Something made me do it.'

'Who? What made you do it?'

'I don't know.'

This was the case with most of the prisoners. Then I asked,
'Have you been in prison before.'

'Oh yes, three or four times.'

'Why do keep coming back?'

'I don't know, I just keep doing the same thing.'

'Did you want to?'

'No.'

'So, what are you doing here?'

'I don't know. I wish I knew.'

Now I have their attention. Now I can explain the Fall of man,
how they became slaves to sin, and God's answer by sending
Jesus.

I said to them, 'Only Christ can set us free from the bondage and slavery of sin. Salvation is the act of saving us from destruction, delivering us from sin and its consequences; and preserving us for everlasting life. Redemption is salvation from sin, a release by purchase. Jesus redeemed us, He bought us back from Satan by paying a price to deliver us from sin and its penalty. He did this by going to the cross.'

All these prisoners responded to my invitation to receive Jesus as Lord.

So redemption and the gift of salvation is forgiveness of sin and deliverance from sin. And the gift of righteousness is freedom from sin as we die to the desires of the flesh and take up our cross and follow Him.

> *'But of Him you are in Christ Jesus, who became for us wisdom from God – and righteousness and sanctification and redemption.'*
> (1 Corinthians 1:30)

> *'Therefore, if anyone is in Christ, he is a new creation, old things have passed away; behold, all things have become new.'*
> (2 Corinthians 5:17)

Jesus is our salvation, redemption, righteousness and true freedom:

> *'... but He whom God raised up saw no corruption. Therefore let it be known to you, brethren, that through this Man is preached to you the forgiveness of sins, and by Him everyone who believes is justified from all things from which you could not be justified by the law of Moses.'* (Acts 13:37–39)

Jesus is our true freedom from everything from which we could not be freed by the Law of Moses; freedom from sin, freedom from eternal death, freedom from every clutch of the devil, freedom to live in Christ.

'For if by the one man's offence death reigned through the one, much more those who receive abundance of grace and of the gift of righteousness will reign in life through the One, Jesus Christ.'

(Romans 5:17)

For freedom Christ has set us free, so let us receive and pursue the gift of righteousness every day of our lives so that God may raise us up in freedom in Him, over every sin, for if the Son sets you free, you are free indeed.

Some Questions to Think About

- What happens when we pursue righteousness?
- Explain the difference between Law and Grace.
- Name three things we should do to live in righteousness.
- What will be the results of living in righteousness?

George (on left) comes home

The Power of Prayer

Prayer is communion with God. There is prayer that bounces off the ceiling and there is prayer that penetrates the heart of God. There is prayer that accomplishes little and there is prayer that effects great change. James 5:16–18 tells us:

> 'Confess your trespasses to one another, and pray for one another, that you may be healed. The effective, fervent prayer of a righteous man avails much. Elijah was a man with a nature like ours, and he prayed earnestly that it would not rain; and it did not rain on the land for three years and six months. And he prayed again, and the heaven gave rain, and the earth produced its fruit.'

The first necessity to having your prayers answered is to live a **righteous life that effects great change**.

In Exodus 32:31–34 we read of Moses pleading with God:

> 'Then Moses returned to the LORD and said, "Oh, these people have committed a great sin, and have made for themselves a god of gold! Yet now, if You will forgive their sin – but if not, I pray, blot me out of Your book which You have written."
>
> And the LORD said to Moses, "Whoever has sinned against Me, I will blot him out of My book. Now therefore, go, lead the people to the place of which I have spoken to you. Behold, My Angel shall

go before you. Nevertheless, in the day when I visit for punishment, I will visit punishment upon them for their sin."'

Moses stood in the gap for the people of Israel, and God answered his prayer immediately.

We too must **stand in the gap** for individual people, our city, for nations.

1 Kings 18:36–39 tells of Elijah's conversation with God:

> *'And it came to pass, at the time of the offering of the evening sacrifice, that Elijah the prophet came near and said, "LORD God of Abraham, Isaac, and Israel, let it be known this day that You are God in Israel and I am Your servant, and that I have done all these things at Your word. Hear me, O LORD, hear me, that this people may know that You are the LORD God, and that You have turned their hearts back to You again." Then the fire of the LORD fell and consumed the burnt sacrifice, and the wood and the stones and the dust, and it licked up the water that was in the trench. Now when all the people saw it, they fell on their faces; and they said, "The LORD, He is God! The LORD, He is God!"'*

Take responsibility to make it happen as Elijah did. God loves it when you trust Him, when you step out in faith, even as Elijah did, at the risk of the Baal worshippers killing him if his God did not answer. His God did answer, with fire that burned up the sacrifice. Elijah had faith. We too must pray with **faith**.

We read of Daniel's petition to the Lord in Daniel 9:3–6:

> *'Then I set my face toward the Lord God to make request by prayer and supplications, with fasting, sackcloth, and ashes. And I prayed to the LORD my God, and made confession, and said, "O Lord, great and awesome God, who keeps His covenant and mercy with those who love Him, and with those who keep His commandments, we have sinned and committed iniquity, we have done wickedly and rebelled, even by departing from Your*

precepts and Your judgments. Neither have we heeded Your
servants the prophets, who spoke in Your name to our kings and
our princes, to our fathers and all the people of the land." '

Daniel prayed, fasting, for the people who had turned away from
God. He was disciplined and prepared for the task ahead, even as
training prepares soldiers for war. We are not fighting flesh and
blood, but principalities of evil. We need to be disciplined and fast
for our land, for those who have turned from God, and fight these
principalities that deceive man, by prayer and *fasting*.

Also read Jonah 3:4–5:

'And Jonah began to enter the city on the first day's walk. Then
he cried out and said, "Yet forty days, and Nineveh shall be
overthrown!" So the people of Nineveh believed God, proclaimed a
fast, and put on sackcloth, from the greatest to the least of them.'

Here you will see the whole of Nineveh saved through the prayer
and fasting of the people, as a result of Jonah's prophecy of doom
as to what would happen if they did not repent.

In 1 Kings 8:28–30 we read part of Solomon's prayer of
dedication of the new temple:

'Yet regard the prayer of Your servant and his supplication, O
LORD my God, and listen to the cry and the prayer which Your
servant is praying before You today: that Your eyes may be open
toward this temple night and day, toward the place of which You
said, "My name shall be there," that You may hear the prayer
which Your servant makes toward this place. And may You hear
the supplication of Your servant and of Your people Israel, when
they pray toward this place. Hear in heaven Your dwelling place;
and when You hear, forgive.'

Solomon cried out to God. Pray specific prayers with meaning.
Pray with urgency. This sometimes gets a very quick answer.

On my first trip to Kenya I experienced such a response from God. When I was told that people were walking four days to receive their healing and that I was going to be the only one praying for them, this made me cry out to God. After all, I had never spoken at a conference before and definitely had never prayed for a group of sick people. I knew I had nothing to give these people and ... what was I doing in the middle of Africa anyway? I cried out to God in tears, 'Jesus, I have nothing to give these people. Only You can do something, only You can heal them. Please help Lord, please heal your people.'

After half an hour of this I suddenly heard His still small voice, and peace began to flood my being. God heard me and He said, 'If I can cry through your eyes like this I can also heal through your hands like this.' That was it, God was going to heal the sick and He did heal the sick. Thirty people were instantly healed that first day and a further 250 people were healed during the next four days.

When we *cry out* to God, He hears our prayer and answers us. In John 4:23 Jesus tells us:

> 'But the hour is coming, and now is, when the true worshipers will worship the Father in spirit and truth; for the Father is seeking such to worship Him.'

Jesus tells us to **pray in spirit and truth**, for such the Father seeks. This is praying in the Holy Spirit, whom the Father gives us.

Isaiah 40:31 encourages us thus:

> 'But those who wait on the LORD
> Shall renew their strength;
> They shall mount up with wings like eagles,
> They shall run and not be weary,
> They shall walk and not faint.'

Be prepared to **wait on the Lord**, for it is here that we renew our strength. We can do nothing, or very little, in our own strength;

but as we daily wait upon the Lord, He gives us all the strength we ever need. Often people tend to wait on the Lord to be more and more filled with His Holy Spirit.

2 Peter 1:1 says:

> *'Simon Peter, a servant and apostle of Jesus Christ, to those who have obtained a faith of equal standing with ours in the righteousness of our God and Saviour Jesus Christ.'*   (RSV)

Our faith is of equal standing as it was in the disciples, so that the Holy Spirit is available to us in all His fullness. However it is up to us to be so yielded to Jesus that our relationship with Him enables more of the fullness of the Holy Spirit to operate in and through our lives. Waiting on God is a time of yielding ourselves fully to His complete love, to then walk with Him in willing obedience. When one walks in willing, even joyful, obedience to the Lord, one finds oneself walking in a new dimension, authority and energy that one could not think possible. For myself, as long as I am walking in Christ, then I know that I can keep walking in this higher dimension, ability and freedom in Him.

> *'Take My yoke upon you and learn from Me, for I am gentle and lowly in heart, and you will find rest for your souls. For My yoke is easy and My burden is light.'*   (Matthew 11:29–30)

> *'Now the Lord is the Spirit; and where the Spirit of the Lord is, there is freedom.'*   (2 Corinthians 3:17, NIV)

Walking in Christ enables the burden to be light as we trust in Him who is so much greater than ourselves.

John 11:33–36 describes what happens after Lazarus had died:

> *'Therefore, when Jesus saw her weeping, and the Jews who came with her weeping, He groaned in the spirit and was troubled. And*

He said, "Where have you laid him?" They said to Him, "Lord, come and see." Jesus wept. Then the Jews said, "See how He loved him!" '

Jesus prayed with **compassion**. This makes who or what you are praying for part of you, making you prepared to go the 'extra mile' to make it happen. Sometimes God is waiting for us to do our part, for Him to do His part. He chose to wait for Elijah to gather the Baal worshippers together and challenge them to build altars to their god and him to build his altar to the Living God. It was then that God answered with fire.

Mark 14:36 lets us in on Jesus' conversation with His Father,

'And He said, "Abba, Father, all things are possible for You. Take this cup away from Me; nevertheless, not what I will, but what You will." '

Jesus prayed that the cup be taken from Him, *'but not My Will, Thy Will.'* Jesus was prepared to be obedient even unto death. We therefore must also **be obedient**.

How do we bring all this together? It is a balance of compassion and taking responsibility to make it happen. The feeling of compassion causes the action. Prayer is not just saying prayers. Prayer is active, effectual, communion with the Living God, who effects the answer. This often causes you to be chosen to effect the answer and become to God an extension of His outstretched hands. God will answer. When we do our part to make it happen, we can be sure that God will do His part to make it happen. To enable God to do His part, we must put God first and love Him first above all things, for when we do this something wonderful happens.

Ephesians 2:6 says:

'... and raised us up together, and made us sit together in the heavenly places in Christ Jesus.'

When He raises us up into the heavenly places, in Him, He gives us the authority of the name of Jesus and the power of the Holy Spirit to cast out sickness, diseases and demons. He gives us authority to heal the sick and to become part of His answer to a lost and dying world.

You and I can effect great change when we really learn how to pray as God would wish us to. When we do this we get to know God, and the more we get to know God, the more we will know that **God will do it**.

Types of Prayer

There are two types of prayer:

1. *Fellowship prayer* – this is where we come to know God more: by coming into His presence in repentance, thanksgiving, praise and worship; by loving Him and waiting on Him, being filled with every spiritual blessing in the heavenly places as it says in Ephesians 1:3:

   'Blessed be the God and Father of our Lord Jesus Christ, who has blessed us with every spiritual blessing in the heavenly places in Christ.'

   We enjoy His love, His joy, and His glorious peace by learning to hear His voice, allowing Him to teach us through Scripture and show us many things.
2. *Intercessory or task prayer* – this is interceding for others, for our cities, for our nations. This can be 'hard work prayer'.

When you bring these two types of prayer together you will realize that fellowship prayer causes intercessory prayer to become reality. You are able to then cry out to God and know that He will answer; you are able to approach Him on behalf of others knowing His love for them. You will be able to pray through to victory, knowing the peace, when you know God has answered. You will be able to hear Him and obey Him by doing your part in the answer, by taking responsibility to make it happen.

Let us rise up and pray. Prayer is more than just bowing the knee; it is bowing in submission to God's will, in sacrificing our own desires to do His will on earth. Let us be part of God's answer to this hurting and needy world. Let us become God's outstretched hand to people God loves, with His love and compassion, which He gives to us freely.

Simply come to God in prayer and allow prayer to become the most exciting, glorious, victorious and challenging fellowship and interaction with our wonderful God, who loves us so much. Action will follow. We don't have to wait to go to Heaven before we can have this fellowship with God.

We can have it now, while we are still here on earth, and go on assignments for Him. When God tells you to do something, *do it* and you will see the answer yourself, for *He is a living God!*

Some Questions to Think About

- What are the two main types of prayer?
- Give areas that help to bring about God's answer.
- What challenges you to begin to pray in earnest?
- What does it mean by doing your part, by taking responsibility to make it happen?

The Lord's Prayer

The Lord's Prayer is the greatest prayer on earth. It is the prayer that Jesus taught His disciples, recorded in the Gospels of Matthew (6:9–13) and Luke (11:2–4) when they asked Him *'Teach us to pray.'* Every denomination uses it; every Christian may have prayed it. It is known throughout the world in most languages, yet we know it so well, have said it so often, that sometimes the meaning and depth of the words are lost.

Our Father

The prayer begins with 'Our Father', not 'My Lord', or 'Our God', but my Father, your Father, 'Our Father'. That is close relationship and only believers can call God 'our Father'. Unbelievers cannot call God 'my Father'. So in order to say the first words it is necessary to accept Jesus as our personal Saviour, and God as our real Father, who created us and loved us even before we were born.

Who art in Heaven

Not somewhere on earth, but in Heaven. Now Jesus would not have taught us to say, 'Our Father who art in Heaven', unless it was possible to get there. How? It means that it is actually possible to come into the heavenly realm in prayer, whilst we are still alive on this earth. We can access Heaven in prayer and come up above the limitations of our lives into the unlimited, supernatural presence of our living Almighty God and Father in prayer.

Hallowed be Thy Name

One can greet our Father in Heaven. This means we can talk to Him. We can meet Him, worship Him, and tell Him how much we love Him. We can thank Him for all He has done for us. We can praise Him for who He is. In order to come into His presence and speak to Him, it is necessary to come to Him through the cross, to ask the Holy Spirit to search our hearts and to confess any sin, so that we may be forgiven. We can then come through thanksgiving and praise right into the presence of God and relate to Him, speak to Him and listen for Him to speak to us.

Thy Kingdom Come

Where? Here on earth, of course, starting in my life, your life, our lives. How? By receiving Him into our lives, opening ourselves more and more to His glorious presence to fill us, by letting Him into every part of our being. By asking Him into our hearts to enable us to come much closer to Him. By asking Him into our minds so that we begin to feel and see life as Jesus sees life, to have His love and compassion for others, to understand others as He does, to allow Him to change our attitudes and our thinking, to ask Him into our bodies so that we begin to walk through life as He walked, going where He wants us to go, serving others for His sake with our hands, to speak forth His words that He specifically gives through our mouths, to simply live for Him in every way.

Thy Will Be Done

In my life first, and then through my life to others. We need to allow Him into our past, to heal all the hurt, traumas, disappointments etc. to then heal us emotionally, mentally, spiritually and physically in every way, to allow Him into our weak areas to make us strong in our weakness.

On Earth as it is in Heaven

How? Through our lives, now healed, prepared and equipped by the Lord Himself. 'Thy Kingdom come, Thy will be done on earth as it is in Heaven!!' How? *Through our lives*. Only believers can go up into the heavenly realm to bring the love of Heaven, the joy of Heaven, the peace of Heaven, the healing of Heaven, the miracles of Heaven down to earth to give them out to others. No one else can. If we don't go daily up into the heavenly places in prayer, to receive these wonderful things from Heaven, to give out to our needy world, no one else can. Nobody else will and the world will be worse off because of it.

Ephesians 1:3 exclaims:

> 'Praise be to the God and Father of our Lord Jesus Christ, who has blessed us in the heavenly realms with every spiritual blessing in Christ.'   (NIV)

This tells us that God has blessed us with every spiritual blessing in the heavenly places. Having received from our Father every spiritual blessing in the heavenly places, we can bring these down to earth into our lives and then, as we do the Father's will on earth, His will shall be done on earth as it is in Heaven, through our lives.

We can become so full of our Father's heavenly blessings, so full of the Holy Spirit, that we begin to serve our Father on earth without even giving it a thought, because we have allowed Him to change us, renew us and fill us with *Himself*. It is then that the gifts of the Holy Spirit begin to operate through our lives through healing or prophecy or teaching, or any other ministry that the Lord wants us to bring to mankind on earth.

Give us this day our daily bread

When we live for God we do not have to worry so much as to how we will live, for we have already brought the blessing into our daily lives and businesses. Our daily bread, though, is not just the physical bread that we eat, but also the spiritual bread that is needed for our spiritual being. Just as our body needs daily food to eat, our spiritual being also needs the daily bread that only the Lord can give to us in prayer:

> *'Jesus said to them, "My food is to do the will of Him who sent Me, and to finish His work. Do you not say, 'There are still four months and then comes the harvest'? Behold, I say to you, lift up your eyes and look at the fields, for they are already white for harvest!"'*   (John 4:34–35)

This speaks of another food and that is doing the Father's will. Somehow doing the Father's will brings a sense of fulfilment that no other work on earth can ever give us.

And forgive us our trespasses as we forgive those who trespass against us

This is so important, as God can only forgive us if we forgive others. Our forgiveness should be **total**. One day the disciples asked Jesus, 'How many times must I forgive my brother?' Jesus turned to them and said 'seventy times seven.' Well, when we have counted up that lot, we will surely lose count!

Forgiveness keeps you free. Any unforgiveness in our lives will hinder us and may even prevent us from receiving healing from God. It is therefore of great importance to make the choice to forgive, and that also means to forgive yourself.

And lead us not into temptation but deliver us from evil

Making a choice to stand firm for Jesus and never to yield to sin will cause temptation to weaken and gives place to victory. Righteousness in Jesus is victory over all evil. When we stand strong against every temptation, we will be delivered from evil. Isaiah 54:14 says:

> *'In righteousness you shall be established;*
> *You shall be far from oppression, for you shall not fear;*
> *And from terror, for it shall not come near you.'*

For thine is the Kingdom, the power and the glory forever and ever. Amen

In Revelation 11:15 we read these marvellous words:

> 'Then the seventh angel sounded: And there were loud voices in heaven, saying, "The kingdoms of this world have become the kingdoms of our Lord and of His Christ, and He shall reign forever and ever!"'

We finish as we began, praising our Father in Heaven for who **He is**! **For His alone is the Kingdom, all power, all glory, forever and ever. Amen.**

It is not enough to just say the prayer, we need to live the prayer. As we live the Lord's Prayer every day of our lives we come to live in the glorious intimacy, protection, victory and blessing of that prayer in our everyday lives. The Lord's Prayer covers the basics of our prayer life while on earth. Let us live the glorious life to which Jesus calls us to live in His presence in the heavenly realm while we are still alive on earth.

Some Questions to Think About

- Why does the Lord's Prayer start with 'Our Father'?
- 'Which art in Heaven' – how can we access Heaven while still walking on this earth?
- 'Thy Kingdom come' – in what areas of our personal lives should His Kingdom come within us?
- 'Thy Will be done on earth as it is in Heaven' – How?
- 'And lead us not into temptation but deliver us from evil' – These statements show that it is very important for us to live in full righteousness. Why?

Equipped to Serve

We are called by God to serve Him. Many are called but few are chosen, as it tells us in Matthew 22:14:

> *'For many are called, but few are chosen.'*

What brings about the change from being called to being chosen? Romans 1:1–6 says:

> *'Paul, a bondservant of Jesus Christ, called to be an apostle, separated to the gospel of God which He promised before through His prophets in the Holy Scriptures, concerning His Son Jesus Christ our Lord, who was born of the seed of David according to the flesh, and declared to be the Son of God with power according to the Spirit of holiness, by the resurrection from the dead. Through Him we have received grace and apostleship for obedience to the faith among all nations for His name, among whom you also are the called of Jesus Christ.'*

Paul was called by God to be set apart for the gospel of God. He had to be set apart from worldly things and ways so that he could live in full righteousness and holiness.

In obedience of faith, for the sake of His name among the nations, include yourselves who are called, to **belong** to Jesus

Christ. Once we **live** Romans 1:1–6, we come to be His chosen, to reach out to the world around us with His glorious gospel.

Spending time daily in His presence is therefore the most important thing you can do, for here you can hear God, hear His call on your life and directions to walk in. In a vision, sometime ago, I saw Jesus and He pointed me to the Father. I took a step in that direction and found myself in a white mist. I could see nothing, I could hear nothing, but what I felt changed my life forever.

I felt just one tiny touch of the Father's heart for the nations of the world. The pain, the love, the sorrow, was so great that I burst into tears. 'I'm sorry', I repeated over and over. What else could I do?

I then realized that half the world seems not to *want* to know Who created them; and many who do often prefer their own chosen lifestyles rather than to turn to Jesus. God is heartbroken, watching the devil steal, kill, and destroy so many humans whom He loves so much and yet so few of His own people are going out with the powerful truth of what Jesus did on the cross to save mankind. Many Christians all over the world are keeping the glorious gospel that Jesus has made available to mankind for themselves only. They sit comfortably in their houses, when millions are dying in their sin, sickness and problems under the grip of the devil.

Many are called, but so few are prepared to go out with the gospel to reach out to the lost for Jesus.

At least fifteen minutes had passed and I was crying bitterly, still saying, *'I'm sorry, I'm sorry.'* Suddenly I knew there was something I could do about it. Even if I am only a girl, there are no excuses. 'Father God,' I prayed, 'I promise You, that from this second on, I will give you every day for the rest of my life to go out to wherever You send me to preach the gospel anywhere You want me to, to rescue as many as I can, out of the clutches of the Evil One and bring them into Your Kingdom. I will also speak to as many churches as I can, to warn Your people to wake up and do the same, to share Your glorious gospel with as many people as possible.' Suddenly I was following Jesus up a steep hill and I knew the Father had accepted my promise. My job now is to keep my eyes constantly on Jesus, not looking left or right, but to keep focused on Him, for the path is narrow and steep and there are many boulders in the way. Yet I know that even if I battle to keep up with Jesus, I will make it to the top of the hill, for next, Jesus sat down upon a beautiful white rock, shining like marble and I panted up to Him and knelt in the dust. Now knowing I was at His side, I could take my eyes off Him and bow my head down onto the cold white rock. As I did this, I came out of the vision. This vision was like a covenant with God Himself and I am doing what I promised. God Himself has led me into a very exciting ministry, where I see His hand at work in very powerful ways.

This is reality, more real and more important than anything else, for serving God embraces eternity and the eternal destiny of millions of people. I know that even in the small bicycle ministry I run, that within ten years, by supplying 100 bicycles, mega-phones and Bibles to 100 evangelists a year in Africa, around one million people can be converted and discipled within that time. I also know that this work will succeed. I have no doubt, because the Lord Himself is doing it.

God the Source

The first, most necessary, preparation to serving God effectively is to come to know God, to seek His will and hear His command. The **Father** is the **source** of all things and **Jesus always points to the source**. This is explained in John 5:19:

> *'Then Jesus answered and said to them, "Most assuredly, I say to you, the Son can do nothing of Himself, but what He sees the Father do; for whatever He does, the Son also does in like manner."'*

Do what you see the Father doing.

Coming into His presence is the only way we can ever see what the Father is doing. That is why Jesus spent so much time praying. He spent forty days in the wilderness before He started His ministry, and all night before He chose His disciples. He spent much time drawing aside by Himself to seek His Father. Jesus describes it thus in John 5:30:

> *'I can of Myself do nothing. As I hear, I judge; and My judgment is righteous, because I do not seek My own will but the will of the Father who sent Me.'*

Here Jesus clearly heard all that He was to do and did nothing on His own authority. It is when we do things on our authority that mistakes are made. When we hear God and obey Him it will always work, for God's ways can never fail. Jesus is and was fully God and fully man. He lived a perfect life on this earth, doing only what the Father told Him to do, and everyone Jesus prayed for was healed and delivered. He provides further confirmation in John 12:49:

> *'For I have not spoken on My own authority; but the Father who sent Me gave Me a command, what I should say and what I should speak.'*

Every teaching, every parable that Jesus gave us was from the Father and His teaching is perfect. Now if Jesus, the very Son of God, had to come to the Father to receive every teaching, every parable, how much more should we? In the Gospel of John alone there are over nine scriptures where Jesus says that His teachings and works are from the Father.

How dare any of us try and preach on our own authority. It does not matter how much Bible training we have had, how clever we may be, how entertaining or poetic or how well versed we are in Scripture, on our own authority the words will be empty and will effect little or no change upon our listeners. Yet

when we have been in God's presence and have the commandment from God as to what to say and speak, it does not matter
that we may not be eloquent speakers or that we may stammer;
for the Holy Spirit will speak through our mouths in power and
authority, to reach the hearts of the people before us, to bring
about changed lives. Even as Paul in 1 Corinthians 2:4–5 says:

> *'And my speech and my preaching were not with persuasive
> words of human wisdom, but in demonstration of the Spirit and
> of power, that your faith should not be in the wisdom of men but
> in the power of God.'*

When God tells you to do something and you obey Him then
you will also know, He will confirm the word He has told you to
speak with power and signs following in the demonstration of
the Holy Spirit in your midst.

Jesus the Authority

Once we have learnt to come to the Father, who is the source
of everything we do for Him, Jesus will give us the authority of
His name, the name above all names, the name to which every
sickness, every demon, every spirit has to bow. This victory He
won on the cross. God has now raised Jesus above every dominion,
power and authority and above every name that is named.

Sicknesses have names, demons have names, every spirit has a
name and all have to bow the knee and obey the powerful name
of Jesus. Luke 10:19 encourages us thus:

> *'Behold, I give you the authority to trample on serpents and
> scorpions, and over all the power of the enemy, and nothing shall
> by any means hurt you.'*

The authority of the powerful name of Jesus has been given to us
to use, to tread over the enemy, and nothing shall hurt us.

In Nigeria I was invited to speak in a very depressed town, well known for demon activity. I even felt this heaviness in the church and fought it while waiting to speak. I was determined to fight it off. My name was called and I walked to the lectern. I said my first sentence when suddenly everything went black. About five minutes later I woke up out of unconsciousness on the floor to peer through legs of people pleading the blood of Jesus over me. It all started to come back and I began to shout at the demon trying to strangle me, louder and louder and on the seventh command it left.

I immediately got up off the floor and gave the sermon more powerfully than I ever had in the past. The pastors all stood up in excitement at the victory gained over the demonic forces. They suddenly realized that, in Jesus, we are actually far stronger than the demonic forces that have held back that town for so long. Now the pastors are taking authority, in Jesus' name, over every demonic force and the town is now free, and the churches are growing. I thank the Lord so much for allowing the demon to attack me, for the victory He gave brought us to a new level in Him and made us bold, as *no* demon can hurt us if we are in Jesus.

A further encouragement is found in Acts 4:30:

> '*by stretching out Your hand to heal, and that signs and wonders may be done through the name of Your holy Servant Jesus.*'

When we stretch out our hands to all in the name of Jesus, signs and wonders and healings happen, without even the laying on of hands. When we preach the simple gospel, signs and wonders will follow as we pray in the mighty name of Jesus.

Often in Africa, when there are three or four hundred sick people, I just tell them to put their own hands on their sickness or pain. I then pray, 'In the name of Jesus: sickness go, in the name of Jesus: pain go, in the name of Jesus: bodies be healed.' Suddenly squeals and shouts of joy speak of a few hundred

Hundreds receive their healing in Soroti Refugee Camp, Uganda

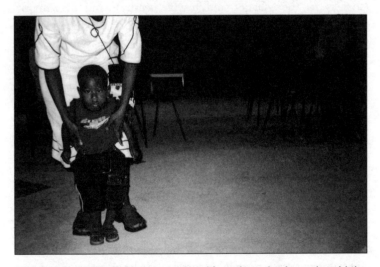

Three-year-old Tando Molipa, paralysed from the waist down since birth,
is able to stand and walk for the first time

receiving their healings right where they are in their seats in Jesus' name.

All I have done is spoken the word in Jesus' name and stretched out my hands towards the people, and Jesus has done the rest! He has healed the people. Jesus is at work today through hundreds of evangelists who can tell you similar stories. Jesus is alive and Jesus is doing it!

The Power of the Holy Spirit

Jesus tells his disciples in Acts 1:8:

> *'But you shall receive power when the Holy Spirit has come upon you; and you shall be witnesses to Me in Jerusalem, and in all Judea and Samaria, and to the end of the earth.'*

The first and most important reason that the 'Holy Spirit and power' is given to us is to enable us to be witnesses for Jesus: first to Jerusalem (that is the local city where we live), then to Judea (that is to the villages and towns nearby), and to Samaria (reaching further afield from our area) and then to the ends of the earth. We should all be witnesses for Jesus with the gifts He has given to us, to reach out to the lost, to bring them out of the clutches of evil into the Kingdom of God.

My job for thirty-five years was to teach horse riding. People ride horses for different reasons, pleasure, company, competition, freedom etc. Horse riders are often a people group searching for something. Horses are the key to this people group. We found a way to reach them for Jesus, through horses, one at a time. This was my Jerusalem experience, leading many to Jesus through my job as a riding teacher. I then wrote *The Biblical Approach to Riding* and have been training riding instructors in this approach in England, the USA and certain countries in Europe, right up to now. This approach to horsemanship has also been shown on national TV in England.

Romans 15:13 gives encouragement to all who trust in Jesus:

> *'Now may the God of hope fill you with all joy and peace in believing, that you may abound in hope by the power of the Holy Spirit.'*

The Holy Spirit is also given to us to fill us with His love, joy and peace in believing that, by the power of the Holy Spirit, we may abound in hope.

God's love, joy and peace fills our hearts, but we must not just seek the Lord for these feelings and keep them for ourselves. We need to go out and do God's work, in whatever area He has gifted us in, as soldiers ready to go out in total obedience to whatever or wherever He is directing us.

This takes obedience, for sometimes we may not want to go to where God wants us to go, to where the need is. Extreme heat and humidity is what I struggle with. I don't mind where I sleep or what I eat, but I don't like humidity, especially where there are no fans or running water for relief. However, I still have to go, and will go. When God heals the sick, it all becomes worthwhile.

John 16:13–15 gives further guidance from Jesus:

> *'However, when He, the Spirit of truth, has come, He will guide you into all truth; for He will not speak on His own authority, but whatever He hears He will speak; and He will tell you things to come. He will glorify Me, for He will take of what is Mine and declare it to you. All things that the Father has are Mine. Therefore I said that He will take of Mine and declare it to you.'*

When you go out in the name of Jesus, know that the Holy Spirit goes with you. He will declare to you all truth, for even He does not speak on His own authority but whatever He hears from the Father. He will take the things of Jesus and declare them to you, even things that are to come. We have everything we ever need to do God's work because ***Jesus is everything we ever need!***

Therefore we shall succeed for Jesus comes with us in the person of the Holy Spirit.

'. . . *in mighty signs and wonders, by the power of the Spirit of God.*'   (Romans 15:19)

We need to go in the power of the Holy Spirit and in the name of Jesus to save, heal and deliver, and God's miracle power becomes reality. We need to go to:

- the Father who is our source
- Jesus who gives us the authority of His name
- the Holy Spirit who equips us with power

Some Questions to Think About

- Why does Jesus point us to the Father?
- What does the authority of Jesus' name accomplish?
- Name three things that the power of the Holy Spirit does.
- If you are equipped by the Father, Son and Holy Spirit, what will you be able to do for God?

The Spiritual Realm and the Holy Spirit

In Uganda I experienced the power of God in a new way when I saw, with my own eyes, the Holy Spirit moving in healing power. Three hundred people were healed within two minutes.

What had I seen the Lord do that day?

I hid my face in my arms as I suddenly saw the spirit realm far more real than the material realm. I saw that sicknesses and healings were controlled more from the spirit realm than the material earthly realm. I realized sickness was sent from the spiritual realm of evil and healing was sent, via the spiritual realm, through Jesus by His victory that He gained by dying on the cross and rising in total and complete victory over every sin, sickness and demonic power in the spirit realm.

This experience made me realize that everything in the material earthly realm has a life span. This life span is controlled by time. Everything on earth is temporary: wood rots, steel rusts, fabrics decay, even our bodies have to die, just like those of all the animals, fish, plants and insects. Everything on earth is controlled by a time span. The earth rotates on its axis, revolving around the sun, giving days, months and years. This gives us day and night. Day and night give us our time span.

The Lord lives outside the span of time. To Him a thousand years are but a day. He lives in the spiritual realm outside the span of time.

When a person prays, he reaches above the time controlled limits of his own earthly realm into the eternal, spiritual, supernatural realm of God's holy and heavenly presence. In God's presence we find His peace, joy, and the covering of His great love for us. Ephesians 1:3 says:

> *'Blessed be the God and Father of our Lord Jesus Christ who has blessed us in Christ with every spiritual blessing in the heavenly places.'*   (NRSV)

This is talking about spiritual blessings in the heavenly places, not physical blessings in the earthly places where we are living. Without Christ, man seeks the physical pleasures in the earthly realm, but in Christ through prayer we can be blessed with much higher spiritual blessings in the heavenly places in Christ Jesus.

> *'I said, "Let days speak,*
> *   and many years teach wisdom."*
> *But it is the spirit in a man,*
> *   the breath of the Almighty, that makes him understand.'*
>   (Job 32:7–8, NRSV)

The earthly physical realm is likened to a smaller racing wheel of time. The heavenly realm is likened to a large slow moving wheel of the universe.

In prayer it is possible to rise up above the racing wheel of one's own life and enter the still, quiet, timeless realm of God's heavenly presence. Here you can hear the Lord speak to you. Here He will teach you to walk in the Spirit, to be led by His Spirit while on earth.

I had to go to Pakistan during a difficult time, but because the Lord spoke to me and led me by His Spirit, I was able to go. At the airport He said to me, 'I have called you and I will not forsake you.' This word gave me the courage to go.

> *'Not by might, nor by power, but by my spirit, says the* LORD *of hosts.'*   (Zechariah 4:6, NRSV)

Romans 8:2–6 explains this more:

> *'For the law of the Spirit of life in Christ Jesus has set me free from the law of sin and death.'*   (verse 2)

So we have free choice to choose how we should live and the fruits of our decision will show in our lives.

Always check the fruit of any organization or system before getting involved in it. The fruit will show what lies behind it, good or evil.

The chart on p. 94 will help to distinguish between the fruits of the Holy Spirit and those of evil. You will see these fruits influencing our lives on earth. All the above are fruits of the Spirit, below are the fruits of evil. Either the fruits of the Holy Spirit or the fruits of evil will show through a person's life, depending on the way they have chosen to live.

What is within us will show through our lives. If evil is within, a negative fruit of anger, hate, envy, or pride may show forth through our physical lives. If the Holy Spirit is within, then peace, joy, and love will show through our lives. Negative fruits showing through our lives can lead to sickness or other bondages, whereas the fruits of the Holy Spirit can lead to health, freedom, joy and peace.

The gifts of the Holy Spirit are also given from the spiritual realm as God has made them available to us. Nine of the gifts are:

> *3 vocal gifts*   – tongues, interpretation of tongues and prophecy
> *3 wisdom gifts* – knowledge, discernment of spirits, wisdom
> *3 practical gifts* – faith, healings and working of miracles

Everlasting Spiritual Heavenly Realm

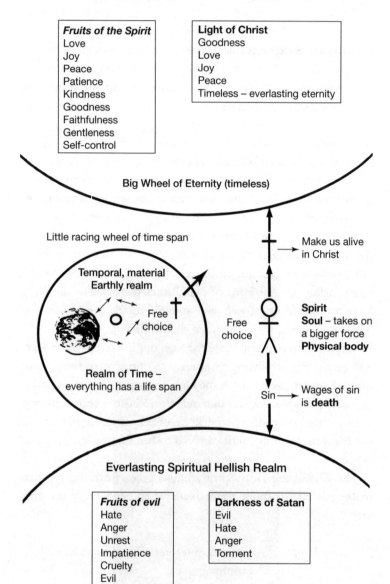

Fruits of the Spirit
Love
Joy
Peace
Patience
Kindness
Goodness
Faithfulness
Gentleness
Self-control

Light of Christ
Goodness
Love
Joy
Peace
Timeless – everlasting eternity

Big Wheel of Eternity (timeless)

Little racing wheel of time span

Temporal, material Earthly realm

Free choice

Realm of Time – everything has a life span

Free choice

Make us alive in Christ

Spirit
Soul – takes on a bigger force
Physical body

Sin ⟶ Wages of sin is **death**

Everlasting Spiritual Hellish Realm

Fruits of evil
Hate
Anger
Unrest
Impatience
Cruelty
Evil
Unfaithfulness
Roughness
Out of control

Darkness of Satan
Evil
Hate
Anger
Torment

None of these gifts is of the earthly realm, they are all spiritual gifts of the Holy Spirit operating from the heavenly spiritual realm, but affecting the physical realm.

Jesus had authority and power over the natural realm by walking on water, calming the storm, turning water into wine and feeding 5,000 people with five loaves and two fishes. He worked miracles over creation. He also cast out demons and healed the sick. He raised the dead. Jesus also had knowledge, discernment of spirits and great wisdom.

Once Jesus ascended into Heaven He poured out His Holy Spirit upon those in the Upper Room on the Day of Pentecost, and from that time on the disciples moved in the gifts of the Holy Spirit, which were given to them to reach the world.

Down through the ages many great men of God have also moved in all the gifts of the Holy Spirit and these same gifts are available for us today.

It is up to us. We can stay in the earthly realm within the laws of nature. Or we can rise up in prayer to where Jesus is seated at the right hand of the Father, above all rule and authority and above every name that is named. In His name you can live above the laws of nature in the higher realm of the supernatural in Christ Jesus.

We were driving through the bush veldt of Northern Ghana at night. I was watching out for any wild animals from the bus when suddenly I saw something horrendous. As tall as a tree, swirling red dust was moving slowly, and a dreadful sense of evil came from it. I began to pray in tongues. It was a figure with the arms outstretched, but it was the folds of dust moving at walking pace that scared me, as it was impossible for dust to move like that naturally.

'Look at that!' I said to Rev. David Botchway beside me.

'Oh that, that is a dust demon, a fallen angel. The locals call them gods and often consult them on various matters. You must not walk in such lonely dark forests at night. They can attack you.'

'But I have never seen or heard of such a thing!' I spluttered.

'The fallen angels seek out the dark and lonely places,' he replied. 'They are not often seen.'

'Fallen angels,' I thought, 'as big as the trees, about 15 feet tall. Angels of God are also that big, but I've never seen an angel of God, yet I've just seen this!!'

Fallen angels!? Thrown out of heaven for their sin!? Fallen man! All because Adam and Eve traded the lovely pre-Fall world and ourselves in exchange for the Knowledge of Good and Evil. Through this we are fallen men and women, just like that fallen angel, walking through the swirling red dust, still alive, fallen from God's grace and heavenly beauty to now walk in darkness and filth, loneliness and rejection. Then I saw more clearly the power of the cross and what Jesus has done for us to save us from eternal darkness and give us a second chance for eternal life with Him.

We have to preach this gospel. We must not deprive people of eternal life through our own laziness, lack of commitment, or lack of caring. We can help in some way to spread this gospel if not by going ourselves, or we can support those who do go.

I challenge you seriously. We all have to stand before God one day. What have we done about the last thing Jesus told us to do before He ascended into Heaven? It is up to us if we don't go or help others to go. No one else will.

> 'And Jesus came and spoke to them, saying, "All authority has been given to Me in heaven and on earth. Go therefore and make disciples of all the nations, baptizing them in the name of the Father and of the Son and of the Holy Spirit, teaching them to observe all things that I have commanded you; and lo, I am with you always, even to the end of the age." Amen.'
>
> (Matthew 28:18–20)

> 'And He said to them, "Go into all the world and preach the gospel to every creature. He who believes and is baptized will be

saved; but he who does not believe will be condemned. And these signs will follow those who believe: In My name they will cast out demons; they will speak with new tongues; they will take up serpents; and if they drink anything deadly, it will by no means hurt them; they will lay hands on the sick, and they will recover." ' (Mark 16:15–18)

'Then He said to them, "These are the words which I spoke to you while I was still with you, that all things must be fulfilled which were written in the Law of Moses and the Prophets and the Psalms concerning Me." And He opened their understanding, that they might comprehend the Scriptures. Then He said to them, "Thus it is written, and thus it was necessary for the Christ to suffer and to rise from the dead the third day, and that repentance and remission of sins should be preached in His name to all nations, beginning at Jerusalem. And you are witnesses of these things. Behold, I send the Promise of My Father upon you; but tarry in the city of Jerusalem until you are endued with power from on high." ' (Luke 24:44–49)

Serving the Lord does cost, but Jesus went all the way to the cross for us. I know that I have to do my utmost for Him, for this is the reality of life.

Let us wake up the churches to reality and do what Christ has commanded us to do. Each one of us is called, each one of us has our special part in it, no matter how big or how small, God does not judge by size, but by the heart. Nor does it matter where the area of service is. It can be right on the very street or area where we live, for not all of us are able to go to the ends of the earth.

There are still many places in this world not yet reached with the gospel and these are the rural villages in isolated areas and to this mission I have pledged myself to God for the rest of my life.

The Gifts of the Holy Spirit

There is much confusion over the gifts of the Holy Spirit, yet if we go to the Bible for our instruction we will discover they are simply supernatural gifts given to us from God to enable us to do His work on earth effectively. Each gift is extremely important and each complements the other gifts. We are given these gifts, and they come into effect when and where they are needed.

Let us take a basic look at each of the nine gifts previously mentioned, starting with the *three vocal gifts*:

1. *Tongues*. Tongues are languages given to us, and may be languages spoken in the world, historic languages, or even those used by angels. They are given to enable us to:

    (a) worship the Lord better – when words are inadequate, tongues enable us to come into a higher realm of worship that brings us closer to the Lord.

    (b) pray for someone when we don't know how to pray – the Holy Spirit will give us the right words to pray for them.

    (c) pray as the Holy Spirit gives utterance in a group of believers.

2. *Interpretation of tongues*. This gift is given in order to interpret a tongue given in public into a known language. Doing so, helps to build up the church as a message from the Lord is heard.

3. *Prophecy*. This is a word from the Lord given in a known language for building up the church.

Then there are *three wisdom gifts* that complement the vocal gifts:

1. *Discernment*. This gift is given to enable us to discern whether a tongue or other word is from God or another source. It enables the church to be built up and provides protection from evil sources.

2. *Knowledge*. This gift can sometimes be used in conjunction with the other gifts. For example, when praying for a sick

person the Lord may give a word of knowledge as to the cause of the sickness. During a prayer meeting a word of knowledge may be given, which may be a warning, an encouragement, or anything that the Lord wants His people to know.

3. *Wisdom*. This gift enables us to know how to handle a specific situation. King Solomon asked God for this gift and received it.

There are then the *three practical gifts*:

1. *Healings*. This gift (plural) may operate through the laying on of hands and can involve anointing with oil. As words of healing are spoken out in the name of Jesus, people are healed from sickness and pain.
2. *Working of miracles*. This gift enables the working of miracles in Jesus' name.
3. *Faith*. This gift enables faith for a specific healing or for whatever the Lord is asking us to do.

Sometimes the Lord may use more than one of the gifts of the Holy Spirit during a healing or miracle.

Some Questions to Think About

- What is the difference between the worldly realm and spiritual realm?
- How does the spiritual realm affect the worldly realm?
- Why are the gifts of the Holy Spirit so important?
- Why is obeying the commandment to 'Go, make disciples of all nations' so important?

The Blessings of Obedience

We all struggle with distress, problems or difficulties in life. Deuteronomy 4:30 says:

> *'When you are in distress, and all these things come upon you in the latter days, then you turn to the LORD your God and obey His voice . . .'*

What brings us into distress? The disobedience of man, when men disobey the Word of God and go their own way. Just as Adam and Eve disobeyed God and brought the world into sin and judgment, so too shall disobedience bring distress and difficulties into the world and God will allow it. Romans 5:19 tells us:

> *'For as by one man's disobedience many were made sinners, so also by one Man's obedience many will be made righteous.'*

Obedience has great consequences; disobedience leads to sin and death. Obedience leads to righteousness and life. We all need to learn obedience, even as Jesus:

> *'though He was a Son, yet He learned obedience by the things which He suffered. And having been perfected, He became the author of eternal salvation to all who obey Him.'*
>
> (Hebrews 5:8–9)

Jesus' obedience to the Father has given us salvation and eternal life.

> *'And being found in appearance as a man, He humbled Himself and became obedient to the point of death, even the death of the cross.'* (Philippians 2:8)

> *'And having been perfected, He became the author of eternal salvation to all who obey Him.'* (Hebrews 5:9)

Jesus was perfectly obedient to the Father. His obedience has secured our victory in Him when we become obedient to Him. We must be obedient to the Father, even as Jesus was. He never did anything, except what the Father told Him. In John alone eleven times it speaks of Jesus only doing what the Father commanded. How much more should we? These following passages from John show Jesus' relationship with God in prayer.

John the Baptist said:

> *'. . . A man can receive nothing unless it has been given to him from heaven.'* (John 3:27)

> *'Then Jesus answered and said to them, "Most assuredly, I say to you, the Son can do nothing of Himself, but what He sees the Father do, for whatever He does, the Son does in like manner."* (John 5:19)

> *'I can of Myself do nothing. As I hear, I judge; and My judgment is righteous, because I do not seek My own will but the will of the Father who sent Me.'* (John 5:30)

> *'Jesus answered them and said, "My doctrine is not Mine, but His who sent Me. If anyone wills to do His will, he shall know concerning the doctrine, whether it is from God or whether I speak on My own authority. He who speaks from himself seeks his own*

glory; but He who seeks the glory of the One who sent Him is true, and no unrighteousness is in Him." ' (John 7:16–18)

'And yet if I do judge, My judgment is true; for I am not alone, but I am with the Father who sent Me.' (John 8:16)

'Then Jesus said to them, "When you lift up the Son of Man, then you will know that I am He, and that I do nothing of Myself; but as My Father taught Me, I speak these things. And He who sent Me is with Me. The Father has not left Me alone, for I always do those things that please Him." (John 8:28–29)

'I speak what I have seen with My Father, and you do what you have seen with your father.' (John 8:38)

'For I have not spoken on My own authority; but the Father who sent Me gave Me a command, what I should say and what I should speak. And I know that His command is everlasting life. Therefore, whatever I speak, just as the Father has told Me, so I speak.' (John 12:49–50)

'Do you not believe that I am in the Father, and the Father in Me? The words that I speak to you I do not speak on My own authority; but the Father who dwells in Me does the works.' (John 14:10)

'But the Helper, the Holy Spirit, whom the Father will send in My name, He will teach you all things, and bring to your remembrance all things that I said to you.' (John 14:26)

'However, when He, the Spirit of truth, has come, He will guide you into all truth; for He will not speak on His own authority, but whatever He hears He will speak; and He will tell you things to come. He will glorify Me, for He will take of what is Mine and

declare it to you. All things that the Father has are Mine.
Therefore I said that He will take of Mine and declare it to you.'
(John 16:13–15)

Jesus had the Father in Him, we have the Holy Spirit in us. And
we should seek to become more obedient even in the smaller
things and grow in obedience until we reach the finer levels of
obedience. One day in London, I walked past a beggar sitting
with his little brown dog near Victoria Station. Suddenly the
Lord told me to go back and witness to him. I had every excuse
why I did not want to do so. But when I did go back and witness
to him in obedience, he accepted Jesus as his Lord and Saviour. I
thank the Lord that I obeyed.

There is a depth in God, an obedience in God, that brings
absolute victory but to this end we need to pray earnestly. We
face problems in different forms daily. Sometimes we meet with
overwhelming forces of darkness, or hurt, or even death. When
someone dies and we don't know why, we feel helpless and on
our own we are helpless.

But there is Someone who has overcome every problem,
every sickness and has even overcome death itself and this is
Jesus. Jesus knew the Father at such depth that He was able to
overcome death itself.

There is a glimpse of light. In the physical realm I competed in
show jumping. But to face the challenging show jumping course,
one has to know one's horse. You have to build up a relationship
of trust and obedience from your horse through many hours of
patient schooling. It is practising with your horse at home that
determines your success in the show jumping arena. It is the
same with God. We have to come to know God in prayer, and to
learn to hear Him like Jesus did, to the refined levels. We can
then step out in total obedience that leads to victory. Yet some of
the challenges of life are very, very hard, but the harder the
challenge, the greater our dependence on God must be. In Him
alone is victory over every form of darkness the devil can

produce. God alone has the victory and this victory we need to find in Him.

So how do we find this victory in God? Through coming to Him seriously in prayer, meeting with Him, talking to Him, listening to Him. We need to make this connection with our spirit, heart and soul. This means determined prayer, not giving up until we have met with God and He with us. You know it when you have met with the living God and made this glorious connection that enables His light to penetrate your innermost being, His truth that enlightens your mind, His supernatural strength that comes into your very body, His victory that brings a result. For this is all about Him, finding out what He wants and finding His will for you. In seeking His will, you find the victory of your life. This is success, for your victory is in His love as He sets you free to move forth in His love.

What was the result of Jesus' obedience?

> 'But He said to them, "Where is your faith?" And they were afraid, and marvelled, saying to one another, "Who can this be? For He commands even the winds and water, and they obey Him!" '   (Luke 8:25)

> 'Then they were all amazed, so that they questioned among themselves, saying, "What is this? What new doctrine is this? For with authority He commands even the unclean spirits, and they obey Him." '   (Mark 1:27)

> 'Now therefore, amend your ways and your doings, and obey the voice of the LORD your God; then the LORD will relent concerning the doom that He has pronounced against you.'
> (Jeremiah 26:13)

Disobedience leads to disaster, but obedience leads to forgiveness and new life. God delights in obedience, God wants to bless:

'So Samuel said:

> "Has the LORD as great delight in burnt offerings
>   and sacrifices,
> As in obeying the voice of the LORD?
> Behold, to obey is better than sacrifice,
> and to heed than the fat of rams." '   (1 Samuel 15:22)

The apostles say the same in Acts 5:29:

> 'Peter and the other apostles replied: "We must obey God rather
> than men!" '   (NIV)

So what must we do now to obey God?

> 'By this we know that we love the children of God, when we love
> God and keep His commandments . . . For whatever is born of God
> overcomes the world. And this is the victory that has overcome the
> world – our faith.'   (1 John 5:2, 4)

Obedience to God gives us His victory that overcomes the world,
the devil and all evil:

> 'casting down arguments and every high thing that exalts itself
> against the knowledge of God, bringing every thought into
> captivity to the obedience of Christ, and being ready to punish
> all disobedience when your obedience is fulfilled.'
>   (2 Corinthians 10:5–6)

We need to be obedient even at the thought level and not
allow any form of disobedience to enter our minds, for all
disobedience is from the devil, whether spoken or argued by
man or secretly entering in. We have the power of the Holy
Spirit available to us, to throw out every negative thought and
thus stay clean:

> *'Therefore I urge you to reaffirm your love to him. For to this end I also wrote, that I might put you to the test, whether you are obedient in all things.'*   (2 Corinthians 2:8–9)

Love God, for if we love God we will be obedient to Him. We will be tested, but if we truly love God we will be able to resist disobedience and obey God.

> *'Since you have purified your souls in obeying the truth through the Spirit in sincere love of the brethren, love one another fervently with a pure heart.'*   (1 Peter 1:22)

If we love God, God will fill us with His love and also give us love for others. If we love others with God's love it will be natural for us to obey every commandment and so give us a pure heart:

> *'But God be thanked that though you were slaves of sin, yet you obeyed from the heart that form of doctrine to which you were delivered.'*   (Romans 6:17)

What will be the results of obedience? What were the results of the Apostles' obedience?

> *'Then the word of God spread, and the number of the disciples multiplied greatly in Jerusalem, and a great many of the priests were obedient to the faith.'*   (Acts 6:7)

What will be the result for us?

> *'Through Him we have received grace and apostleship for obedience to the faith among all nations for His name, among whom you also are the called of Jesus Christ.'* (Romans 1:5–6)

The victory in obedience is ours. When we are obedient we are guaranteed to be walking in God's way. Abraham was blessed through his obedience. God promised Abraham in Genesis 22:18:

> *'In your seed all the nations of the earth shall be blessed, because you have obeyed My voice.'*

We need to obey by first listening to God. We have to spend time in His presence listening to His Voice and then obey Him. Ask Him daily and He will tell you what to do.

> *'Then the kingdom and dominion,*
> *And the greatness of the kingdoms under the whole heaven,*
> *Shall be given to the people, the saints of the Most High.*
> *His kingdom is an everlasting kingdom,*
> *And all dominions shall serve and obey Him.'* (Daniel 7:27)

This prophecy is for those of us who obey God. When we obey the voice of God we know His will will be done. We are merely men, we have no power of ourselves, but when we obey our most High God, His power, His authority works through our being and miracles and healings are performed in the mighty name of Jesus.

> *'But you are a chosen generation, a royal priesthood, a holy nation, His own special people, that you may proclaim the praises of Him who called you out of darkness into His marvellous light.'*
> (1 Peter 2:9)

Once when I went to Malawi there was a problem with receiving e-mails. We had already paid for our tickets so I got on the plane with nothing properly planned and absolutely no way of getting hold of the pastors I was supposed to work with. I only knew that one pastor lived in a village I know, so I headed there the next day. This pastor had not even received my letter but he was so happy to see us that within two hours we were preaching to a full church.

We had just finished the service when there was a knock on the door. It was the Mozambique Pastor whom the Holy Spirit had led straight to the door. He needed money to set up the crusade the following week and all was arranged.

Next day, we headed for the crusade at Oxford Bible Church, not even knowing in which village it was situated! We headed off in the direction I felt led to, and about three hours later I felt led to slow down as we went through a very small village. Suddenly a bike overtook us and stopped us. They said, 'You have just gone past the meeting place where they arranged to meet you by e-mail.' This e-mail had never arrived, yet we were on time and followed them down a narrow track to 'Oxford Bible Church'!!

The whole trip went so well because it was planned by God and not by us.

Some Things to Think About

- Romans 5:19 – explain this verse.
- What was the result of Jesus' obedience?
- What must we do to obey God?
- What are the results of obedience?

How to Receive and Flow in the Anointing

'For as by a man came death, by a man has come also the resurrection of the dead. For as in Adam all die, so also in Christ shall all be made alive.'   (1 Corinthians 15:21–22 ESV)

You have no choice to be born in the physical, but you do have the choice to be born spiritually and this causes the God of Heaven to become your Father.

As you need lungs to breathe in the physical realm, you also need the Holy Spirit to breathe in the spiritual realm. In Hebrew this is *ruach*, which means 'breath of God'. Breathing brings life into your body and without breathing you die. The Holy Spirit brings eternal life into your spirit and without the Holy Spirit you are spiritually dead.

From the moment a child breathes, he will grow up into the natural realm in the world. Likewise from the moment a person is born of the Holy Spirit, he or she can grow up into Christ in the supernatural heavenly realm.

Now, as any person has within him or her natural gifts to develop and use in life, so too we are given supernatural gifts to grow into and use in the spiritual realm. In the natural realm we need training to develop our gifts, which may become our life work. So too with the supernatural, we need much time in the presence of God daily to develop our spiritual gifts. When we do this, then we receive our anointing from God for the specific task that He has prepared for us.

Finding this anointing and calling from God is the essence of life and brings to us our complete fulfilment, as we have found the very thing that God has created us for, and to become.

Let us go a little deeper and see what the Scripture says. After Adam and Eve had sinned, God spoke:

> 'To the woman He said,
>
>> "I will greatly multiply your sorrow and your conception.
>> In pain you shall bring forth children . . . " '   (Genesis 3:16)

It is amazing that the same chapter and verse number (3:16) appears in John's Gospel to show the pain and suffering Jesus went through to enable us to be reborn to eternal life:

> 'For God so loved the world that He gave His only begotten Son, that whoever believes in Him should not perish but have everlasting life.'

Genesis 3:16 shows us how, in choosing the Knowledge of Good and Evil, Adam and Eve brought pain into the world. And John 3:16 shows us Jesus enduring pain on the cross to deliver us from the dominion of evil.

In the dictionary *pain* means 'bodily or mental suffering', and *suffer* means 'to be subjected to pain by choice or for a reason'. Jesus suffered pain for us.

> 'But we see Jesus, who was made a little lower than the angels, for the suffering of death crowned with glory and honour, that He, by the grace of God, might taste death for everyone.'
>
> (Hebrews 2:9)

What Does This Mean for Us?

> 'For to this you were called, because Christ also suffered for us, leaving us an example, that you should follow in His steps.'
>
> (1 Peter 2:21)

We are called to follow in Christ's footsteps:

> *'Therefore, since Christ suffered for us in the flesh, arm yourselves also with the same mind, for he who has suffered in the flesh has ceased from sin, that he no longer should live the rest of his time in the flesh for the lusts of men, but for the will of God.'*
>
> (1 Peter 4:1–2)

We are called to think like Christ and to die to our human passions:

> *'who Himself bore our sins in His own body on the tree, that we, having died to sins, might live for righteousness – by whose stripes we were healed.'* (1 Peter 2:24)

We are called to die to sin, to die to the old man, to die to the desires of the flesh, to our wants, to the world in spirit, soul and body and then take up our cross and follow Him:

> *'And he who does not take his cross and follow after Me is not worthy of Me.'* (Matthew 10:38)

> *'When He had called the people to Himself, with His disciples also, He said to them, "Whoever desires to come after Me, let him deny himself, and take up his cross and follow Me. For whoever desires to save his life will lose it, but whoever loses his life for My sake and the gospel's will save it. For what will it profit a man if he gains the whole world, and loses his own soul?"'*
>
> (Mark 8:34–36)

In Luke 14:26–27 Jesus says that we should so love God that our love for Mum and Dad and brother and sister should seem like hatred compared with the love we have for the God who gave those loved ones to us. It is a measure of *comparative* disregard, not an excuse to break the fifth of the Ten Commandments to honour your father and mother etc.:

> *'If anyone come to Me and does not hate his father and mother, wife and children, brothers and sisters, yes, and his own life also, he cannot be My disciple. And whoever does not bear his cross and come after Me cannot be My disciple.'*

> *'And He, bearing his cross, went out to a place called the Place of a Skull, which is called in Hebrew, Golgotha.'*   (John 19:17)

Jesus went all the way for us. Should we not then be prepared to go full out for Him for the rest of our lives? If Jesus only went half way for us, then salvation would not have been possible. But the result is that Jesus rose from the dead and this result is the same for us as well.

> *'Now if we died with Christ, we believe that we shall also live with Him; knowing that Christ, having been raised from the dead, dies no more. Death no longer has dominion over Him. For the death that He died, He died to sin once for all, but the life that He lives, He lives for God. Likewise you also, reckon yourselves to be dead indeed to sin, but alive to God in Christ Jesus our Lord.'*
> (Romans 6:8–11)

When we have taken that step to die to self, to die to the world, to die to everything we hold dear, to take up our cross and follow Christ, something wonderful happens. ***By putting God first, we no longer limit Him***. The Lord cannot work through the flesh that wants to do its own thing. He cannot work through people who put other things before Him. He cannot work through a sinful nature. All these things limit Him.

God can only work through a person who has died to these things and is surrendered to Him in willing obedience. This person will not limit God but be an open channel for God to work through in power. ***On this person the anointing of God will dwell***.

But someone asked, 'If these are all free gifts from God, how can you now earn or deserve them?' But consider a Learjet; it would be useless as a free gift to you unless you learnt how to fly it, obeyed the rules of physics etc. Our Bible is our instruction manual for the anointing which the Lord has given to us. And you have to put fuel into the fuel tank. Then you have to have faith for the jet to take off into the air. So with the anointing, you have to put much prayer in, if you want to take off in the Holy Spirit and fly in the anointing. Yes, we *are* given free gifts but it takes faith and action to move in them, for God's power is only released as we walk in Him in obedience and faith, having first drenched our task ahead in prayer. *Then* we will see results, for the anointing God gives to us is far more valuable than a Learjet.

What Will the Results Be?

1. We can become an instrument of God to the nations
Let's see what God says to Cyrus:

> 'Thus says the LORD to His anointed,
> To Cyrus, whose right hand I have held –
> To subdue nations before him
> And loose the armour of kings,
> To open before the double doors,
> So that the gates will not be shut:
> "I will go before you
> And make the crooked places straight;
> I will break in pieces the gates of bronze
> And cut the bars of iron." '   (Isaiah 45:1–2)

When we receive the anointing of God and obey Him, God can do anything He wants through us. We will suddenly see success in all He tells us to do and He will do more through us than we can think or imagine. I am speaking to you, not just from the Bible but also from my own experience. I was just a children's riding teacher for thirty-five years, yet when I died to self to follow Jesus wholeheartedly, doors began to open and the next thing I knew, I found myself becoming an international evangel-ist, writing books, going on television and people were wanting to hear me preach. Now, let me tell you, I cannot preach, but I do hear God so I simply speak what He gives me to say! It is *His* words that bring results; it is *His* words that people want to hear!

2. We receive teaching from the Lord

> *'But the anointing which you have received from Him abides in you, and you do not need that anyone teach you; but as the same anointing teaches you concerning all things, and is true, and is not a lie, and just as it has taught you, you will abide in Him.'*
>
> (1 John 2:27)

The anointing of the Holy Spirit teaches us everything we need to say. I have been to Bible College and received much good teaching but, in comparison with that, I have to say that what I have received from God in prayer is of another dimension, a dimension which brings results *far* beyond my own ability! When whole churches respond to the message, I too bow down with them to receive from our wonderful, almighty God, for the words I preach are not my own but those which He has commanded me to say. It is His words that bring such results; they are not my words.

3. We receive understanding

> *'But you have an anointing from the Holy One, and you know all things.'*   (1 John 2:20)

When the Lord teaches us, He also gives us understanding. He opens our minds to His knowledge. He enables us to communic-ate His truths in a way that people can understand easily. We do not need to get any teaching second-hand, we only need to come to Christ to let Him show us what to say.

4. The Lord protects us from the enemy

> '*Do not touch my anointed ones;*
> *do my prophets no harm.*'   (Psalm 105:15, NIV)

5. We can step out in faith, trusting fully in Christ alone

> '*Now He who establishes us with you in Christ and has anointed*
> *us is God, who also has sealed us and given us the Spirit in our*
> *hearts as a guarantee.*'   (2 Corinthians 1:21–22)

6. The task becomes easy

> '*For My yoke is easy and My burden is light.*'
> (Matthew 11:30)

This comes into effect as we totally trust Him and have His abiding peace within, for then God's work gets done without much effort from ourselves. We obey what God tells us to do and He simply does the rest. He does what we cannot do. He moves in power and authority. He moves in the supernatural when healings and miracles simply happen. Suddenly we are moving in this higher realm in Him, trusting in Him alone.

We move from the natural, earthly realm into the supernatural realm. We move from the time realm into the timeless realm, where God's word, spoken at the time of creation, is as powerful now as it was then. God spoke the world into being by His word, and the Bible says in Mark 11:22–24 that if we tell a mountain to be removed, it will be removed. If one does not doubt but *believes* the things one says, *they will be done*. However, this passage tells us that there is first a battle to fight to overcome the obstacles (the mountains) in the way. For example, in India I was asked to pray for a woman with a crushed upper arm as a result of being run over four months ago. Her upper arm was bent and swollen, causing her terrible pain, and her forearm and hand were limp due to weakness from the break. When I saw what I had to pray for, I saw the obstacle – the mountain in my way – a break that was impossible for the doctors to fix. This was a challenge, and the room was filling up with people from the street who had come to watch the miracle. 'Lord, You can do anything!' I was battling. I told doubt to leave in Jesus' name. Suddenly, I moved out of the natural realm into the supernatural realm and faith rose from within me. I began to pray for that arm, which slowly began to straighten. The swelling and pain disappeared and strength returned to the woman's arm and fingers. After a few minutes she was able to move them freely. She was completely healed and the people screamed with delight. I gave them the gospel message and led them all through the sinner's prayer.

Once I had removed the mountain of doubt, I could speak out in faith and watch Jesus do the miracle. We must see by faith and not give in to the flesh which says it cannot be done. Tell doubt to get out of the way, open your mouth and declare it, and it *will* be done.

Do you want to move in this realm? Are you prepared to die to self in order that God can use you? Let us pray:

> Dear Lord, I come to You, search my heart. Forgive me when I have gone wrong. Highlight in me the areas where I must die to self. I choose to die to self that You may live in me and anoint me to do Your work here on earth. I yield myself to You right now. Thank You Jesus. Amen

Now carry on praying and Jesus Himself will minister to you.

Some Questions to Think About

- How did pain come into the world and what did Jesus do about it?
- Explain how to be born into eternal life.
- Why must we die to self?
- What does the anointing enable us to do?

*Mrs C. Padmavathia lifting her arm – no longer broken
but straightened, strengthened and healed*

*People crowding the room to watch Jesus heal the broken arm –
they all became Christians as a result*

Stepping Out in Faith

'The apostles said to the Lord, "Increase our faith!"

He replied, "If you have faith as small as a mustard seed, you can say to this mulberry tree, 'Be uprooted and planted in the sea,' and it will obey you.' " ' (Luke 17:5–6, NIV)

How many of us ask the Lord the same *'Please increase our faith'*? I say it before every meeting I speak at. Just because I have seen the Lord heal many people does not mean that I have much faith. I still need more faith. I still have to ask the Lord to 'increase my faith'.

The Bible speaks of *three* types of faith.

1. Our Faith in Jesus

This involves confessing our sins and receiving Jesus into our lives as Lord and Saviour, and then living our life of faith in Jesus Christ as Lord.

2. Faith in Action or 'Stepping Out in Faith'

This is trusting God to do the things He has promised us, as we preach the gospel, heal the sick, cast out demons and deliver the oppressed. This is the area of faith I ask the Lord for; to increase my faith in the sense meant in Hebrews 11:1–3:

> 'Now faith is the substance of things hoped for, the evidence of things not seen. For by it the elders obtained a good testimony. By faith we understand that the worlds were framed by the word of God, so that the things which are seen were not made of things which are visible.'

This is a tremendous statement, for it shows us that the Word of God is more stable, more concrete, more real than that which is visible, than that of the material realm in which we live. In the material realm we cannot see it. We need to understand this from a higher, spiritual, supernatural realm. After all, 2 Corinthians 5:7 says:

> 'We live by faith, not by sight.' (NIV)

Faith is greater than what we see. It is knowing God's answer before we see it. It is walking in His victory before it arrives. We walk in faith knowing God will do it, not hoping He *might* do it but having heard the answer in prayer, we will then know beyond all doubt that He will do it as we obey Him. We will see this answer unfold before our eyes.

So how do we get faith?

1. We need to know we have received Jesus as Lord by faith with our hearts.

   > 'For by grace you have been saved through faith, and that not of yourselves; it is the gift of God.' (Ephesians 2:8)

2. We need to know Christ dwelling in our hearts. Paul's prayer for the Ephesians was:

   > '. . . according to the riches of His glory . . . Christ may dwell in your hearts through faith; that you, being rooted and grounded

*in love, may be able to comprehend with all the saints what is
the width and length and depth and height – to know the love
of Christ which passes knowledge; that you may be filled with
all the fullness of God.'*   (Ephesians 3:16–19)

How can Jesus dwell in our hearts, that we be grounded in
love and receive strength to comprehend His great love and
become filled with all the fullness of God? Simply by getting
to know God in prayer. The more we wait on God, the
more His Holy Spirit will give us the revelation of His love
and increasingly fill us with His glorious love and presence
until, like Paul, we can say (which is the next stage):

3. By allowing Christ to live in us:

*'I have been crucified with Christ; it is no longer I who live, but
Christ lives in me; and the life which I now live in the flesh I
live by faith in the Son of God, who loved me and gave Himself
for me.'*   (Galatians 2:20)

His love, that took Him to the cross to die in our place,
builds us up and raises us up with Him into a new
dimension of living. His love then opens our eyes to His
reality and victory and the knowledge of His will for us.
This enables us to trust God in a new way.

4. Through prayer and hearing the word of God:

*'Therefore, having been justified by faith, we have peace with
God through our Lord Jesus Christ, through whom also we
have access by faith into this grace in which we stand, and
rejoice in hope of the glory of God.'*   (Romans 5:1–2)

Prayer becomes more and more wonderful as we get to
know God more and more. We have access right into His
presence and grace.

Above all, consider Romans 10:17:

'So then faith comes by hearing and hearing by the word of God.'

5. By becoming rooted and established in our faith. Let us consider Colossians 2:6–7:

   > '*As you have therefore received Christ Jesus the Lord, so walk in Him, rooted and built up in Him and established in the faith, as you have been taught, abounding in it with thanksgiving.*'

   This is not just talking about having faith in God, but being rooted and established in our faith in God; our faith in the sense of living out our faith every day of our lives in every way, in the practical as well as the supernatural.

6. By putting our faith into pratice. No study would be complete without a mention of James 2:14–17:

   > '*What does it profit, my brethren, if someone says he has faith but does not have works? Can faith save him? If a brother or sister is naked and destitute of daily food, and one of you says to them, "Depart in peace, be warmed and filled," but you do not give them the things that are needed for the body, what does it profit? Thus also faith by itself, if it does not have works, is dead.*'

   This is talking about practical faith. We need practical faith then we can move by our obedience into supernatural faith.

7. By facing trials. Another key verse is Ephesians 6:16:

   > '*above all, taking the shield of faith with which you will be able to quench all the fiery darts of the wicked one.*'

   Consider also these verses from James:

   > '*My brethren, count it all joy when you fall into various trials, knowing that the testing of your faith produces patience. But let patience have its perfect work, that you may be perfect and complete, lacking nothing.*' (James 1:2–4)

We need to face the trials of life with the positive faith God gives to us, steadfast and strong so that the problems of life no longer press us down but rather so that we use them as stepping stones into ever more victory, steadfastness and triumph in Christ, so as to:

> *'Fight the good fight of faith, lay hold on eternal life, to which you were also called and have confessed the good confession in the presence of many witnesses.'*   (1 Timothy 6:12)

> *'Therefore we also, since we are surrounded by so great a cloud of witnesses, let us lay aside every weight, and the sin which so easily ensnares us, and let us run with endurance the race that is set before us, looking unto Jesus, the author and finisher of our faith, who for the joy that was set before Him endured the cross, despising the shame, and has sat down at the right hand of the throne of God.'*   (Hebrews 12:1–2)

8. By increasing our faith. Let us reconsider Luke 17:5–6 where the apostles said to Jesus, *'Increase our faith'*:

> *'And the apostles said to the Lord, "Increase our faith." So the Lord said, "If you have faith as a mustard seed, you can say to this mulberry tree, 'Be pulled up by the roots and be planted in the sea,' and it would obey you."'*

What is Jesus actually saying? He is talking about the smallest of seeds, that of a mustard seed that grows into a giant tree. Could He be implying that our faith will grow from a small mustard seed into a giant tree? As I look back on the twenty-five years where I have kept a diary of God's working in my own life, I see this to be true, which is why I have included the testimony of His workings in my life in the last chapters of this book. We have to move in the smaller steps of faith before we move in the bigger steps of faith.

3. The Gift of Faith

A special supernatural gift of faith can come as God gives you a *rhema* word, that is, a specific instruction to do something for Him. I had this experience in Kenya when I knew I would have to pray for a man dying of AIDS. He was so sick that he could not sit up anymore and had to lie on the children's mat in the front of the church.

I asked the Lord, 'What about this man dying of AIDS?'

'I am going to heal him' was the reply.

'How?'

In the Spirit I then saw myself pulling him to his feet. I would never normally do that, but just then I was called forward to pray for this man. As I rose from the church pew, I could feel supernatural faith *surge* within me. I walked straight up to the man and took hold of his hand and, pulling him to his feet, said *'Rise up and walk in Jesus' name.'*

By the time he was on his feet he was healed! This *rhema* word and extra gift of faith was for this particular situation and, as a result of this man's healing, a further 100 people accepted Jesus as Lord. Within a few weeks, this man was back to work with a clear 'HIV negative' certificate from the doctors.

This supernatural gift of faith operates for specific tasks that the Lord has for you, often for the bigger miracle healings. When I hear God say, 'I will heal this person', I tell them so; I tell them, 'Within a few minutes you will be walking.'

In Ghana I told a lady with paralysed knees from arthritis, 'Within a few minutes you will be healed,' and, within a few minutes, she was able to walk up and down steps. (There actually is a video of this on our website: www.standlakeranch.co.uk) On the next day we visited her again and she came to meet us, so excited about her healing.

On another occasion, in Nigeria, a lady paralysed for twenty-two years down one side of her body from a stroke and unable to

*Doris Lattia, healed from arthritis that had paralysed her for over a year,
gets up and walks*

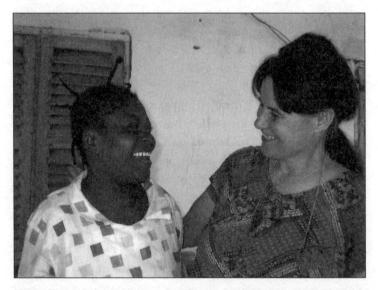

*The next day Doris testifies of her miraculous healing: she was completely
healed from arthritis that had paralysed her for over a year*

speak was healed in $2\frac{1}{2}$ minutes, speaking out in Jesus' name and walking.

To move in the gift of faith, you need first to hear God, believe God and obey God. As you obey God, you will see the miracle unfold.

Let me challenge you by asking, 'Do you *want* to step out in supernatural faith?' After all, Jesus challenged His disciples on several occasions:

> *'But He said to them, "Why are you fearful, O you of little faith?'*
> *Then He arose and rebuked the winds and the sea, and there was*
> *a great calm.'* (Matthew 8:26)

> *'So Jesus answered and said to them, "Have faith in God. For*
> *assuredly, I say to you, whoever says to this mountain, 'Be*
> *removed and be cast into the sea,' and does not doubt in his heart,*
> *but believes that those things he says will be done, he will have*
> *whatever he says. Therefore I say to you, whatever things you ask*
> *when you pray, believe that you receive them, and you will have*
> *them."'* (Mark 11:22–24)

This is yet more counsel from Jesus then to **have faith in God** and **believe that you have received it, and it will be yours**.

On my trip to Kenya in 2005 we visited Kissi, up in the hills, for an outdoor crusade when suddenly rain clouds began to come and the elders came in and said that it was going to rain and spoil the crusade. And I said, 'If God wants the crusade, He can stop the rain.' So we all prayed. Suddenly others came rushing in to the room saying they had just seen the cloud turn around! And yet it was not windy. We had a wonderful crusade in sunlight even though it was raining everywhere else. Through this, the whole village became Christians. And the churches united in evangelism to tell the neighbouring villages that Jesus is truly Lord.

We also need to keep in mind 1 Corinthians 2:4–5:

> '*And my speech and my preaching were not with persuasive words of human wisdom, but in demonstration of the Spirit and of power, **that your faith should not be in the wisdom of men but in the power of God.***'   (emphasis added)

Some Questions to Think About

- What do the '*increase our faith*' verses of Luke 17:5–6 mean to you?
- Describe the word 'faith'.
- Name the three types of faith.
- Where can you step out in faith?

Paralysed from a stroke twenty-two years ago, this lady is healed in Jesus' name, and walks and speaks after two and a half minutes

Spring Valley Riding School – My Jerusalem

Not all of us are able to go out, full-time, and reach the lost. We have to earn a living. We have family, dependants etc. So how do we step out in faith right where we are? There are many ways: getting involved with your church, giving money to evangelists, or setting up something on your own where people can come to you.

This is what we did for many years, and God blessed the work greatly. I could not go out, so ... How could I reach the unchurched? Where could people go if they wouldn't go to a church?

People love sport. People love holidays. People love adventure. These are just some ways of reaching out to people. Find the people group that you know you can reach and reach them through the thing they love, or do the most.

Horse riding was my love, and many love horse riding. So I opened a riding school and used horse riding as a way to bring many to Jesus. This worked so well that I wrote my first book, *The Biblical Approach to Horsemanship*, which then took me to many countries of the world. This was my Jerusalem. Faith then took us from Jerusalem to Judea.

Spring Valley Holiday Farm & Riding Centre – How It All Began

Since the miraculous healing of my horse Jacky Boy in South Africa (detailed in my second book, *Dare to Follow*), I had grown steadily in the Lord. Yet, apart from the witness of Jacky's healing, I was not serving God. I had promised God I would serve Him, and I meant it, so I booked into Bible College for preparation. After one term I had to come back to the riding school. Maybe I was not good enough to be a missionary, or maybe I would have to sell the riding school. But the Lord kept me at the riding school and blessed me abundantly that coming year.

In that one year I had saved seven times more than the normal income. Only God could bless like that, so what must I do with it? The answer came strongly, through a prophecy:

> 'Get to the hills, for lo there cometh rain. The drought is over and past, and the sound of rain approacheth! Yes, I will send showers of blessing upon the hearts of My waiting people, for as they call, I will answer, and while they are waiting upon Me, I shall come down upon them.'

Two weeks later I heard my father on the 'phone. A property set in the hills, for exactly the amount of money saved! I rushed in on him. Others had first option and I immediately asked for a second option. Later, seeing this beautiful piece of land, I asked God if this was the place, and it was as if He said, 'Look in the cowsheds.' In the cowsheds, wooden prefab holiday chalets were stacked in flat-packs, right up to the roof! Yes, this was the place! I went ahead and bought Spring Valley, Maitland (just outside Port Elizabeth, South Africa).

The following month, my future husband Wilfrid returned from Israel, where he had been serving on a kibbutz, and we got married. We had been going out for seven years but I was afraid to get married, so Wilfrid finally wrote from Israel saying, 'Consider yourself engaged.' I didn't consider myself engaged at first but then went to the Bible and the Lord spoke to me that it was right to marry Wilfrid. So we got married in September 1983. We have been happily married ever since.

A month later, Longfield Riding Centre, my previous riding school, which I had been renting for seven years, was sold. So we had a month to close down. We applied for a Christian Camp Site licence for Spring Valley, but were told it would take some time. Wilfrid and I therefore returned to the Bible Institute in Kalk Bay to receive extremely valuable training, and then, as our licence still had not arrived, we went to Israel.

In Israel we helped with the running of a well managed American-based Christian camp and conference centre near Peda-Tikva called *The Baptist Village*. The Lord even opened the way for me to go to England to get a higher Riding Instructor's qualification.

Back home again, the licence was still not through. Maybe we must become missionaries after all. So we went to a month-long Perspective Course run by the Anglican Mission Association, near Pretoria.

After this excellent training, Wilfrid and I made our way to the September Anglican Mission Association Launch Conference in Cape Town. We were uncertain as to whether we ought to leave Spring Valley for a time to 'do missionary service' in South America or immediately develop Spring Valley Centre – as a riding school, on the one hand, and a Christian Centre for missionary training and Youth Outreach on the other? It was at the Conference that the Lord gave us our direction regarding Spring Valley.

We went down to the conference, half-expecting to have to come home, pack our bags, and be off to South America as missionaries. *But God had other plans*. He turned us around, told us to pack our bags and go straight home to Spring Valley, the farm He had given us to open up to His glory, and strangely enough, the place where we most wanted to be!

Since returning, we decided that, as it was totally impossible to do anything without a permit, licence, labour or sufficient money, there was only one thing left we could do and that was to pray. We then left Spring Valley in God's hands and watched Him answer our prayers in the most amazing way.

The very next day an excellent labourer came looking for work. Gibson was the man we needed and soon the farm was beginning to look better. A qualified plumber applied to rent the second cottage and soon became part of the work. The permit that we had been awaiting arrived. We were offered building blocks at a good discount price, we had a gift of a much-needed drill and someone offered to support us for three months so that I could give up my job and concentrate on getting the Riding Centre going.

The Riding Centre was to be the support for the future. A pupil also gave us some walling. There was still the problem of a lack of a labourer's cottage, plus a delay on building the stables, limiting us to five horses. This was because of the space devoted to the Christian centre – so, after a little thought and prayer, we asked our next-door neighbour Abel about leasing some of his land next to our property. He agreed to lease us two hectares, complete with labourer's cottage, for the equivalent of £20 a month. We were suddenly able to keep ten horses. Having sold my own horse to help pay for materials, God provided a gift of another horse within about a week for the riding school.

We re-submitted plans for the stable complex, having stumbled across a Christian architect who offered to do this for half the normal price. The plans were accepted.

All this happened in about two months, culminating with the licence being paid for enabling us to open Spring Valley officially as a Riding Centre. So I was able to build up the centre and to do outreach work amongst the local Xhosa people in our spare time.

We know that the greatest works that God does have been accomplished, **not by human effort, but by human trust in God's effort through prayer**. We thanked the Lord for all He had done, seeking to stay fully in His will. We also thanked our prayer supporters for their backing and asked them to thank the Lord with us.

January 1986

The Lord continued His work at Spring Valley in a most amazing way. Soon I was to realize just how much we would have limited God's power, had I held on to my job through lack of faith.

Almost gaping with surprise, we have seen God supply every need financially, spiritually and practically. For instance, we were in need of a split-pole fence to replace a broken, dangerous wire one; so we prayed about it. Two days later, after church, someone approached us and asked us if we could use some parallel split poles. We accepted gladly. Then someone 'phoned us and offered us some uprights. The next day, we erected a complete fence and the poles were exactly the right number needed.

We were able to buy materials cheaply for the labourer's cottage and Dan moved in. The riding camps were also greatly blessed, as the Lord fulfilled His promise: *'As they wait upon Me so I will come down upon them.'*

The first camp participants were already committed Christians and they grew in faith. On the first night of the second camp participants were upset about the news of a tragedy in which a mine had blown up a family. I therefore shared about the origin of sin, Adam and Eve and the answer to it through Jesus. All eight children gave their lives to Christ.

On Christmas Day I took biscuits over to the Xhosa people. I sat down and told them about how Jesus could be born in their hearts. All five gave their lives to Christ and were so excited, asking if I could teach them more about Jesus. They then continued to come for a weekly Bible Study.

On Boxing Day we had to turn away clients due to lack of horses, so we prayed about it. Four days later we had the gift of a beautiful pony called Challenger. God's timing was perfect. Eight children subsequently made a commitment to Christ.

We tried to mark out the foundations for the stables. This, we discovered, was not so easy, and eventually gave up. Then the following Saturday, a family who we had met only once, turned up with spades and equipment. They said they had been led to pray for us and, as they were praying, the Lord said, 'What about you?' In obedience they had come and, as they were professional builders by trade, they marked out our whole stable complex beautifully. As if this was not enough, they arrived in the same way the following Saturday and dug our complete foundations! What a mighty God we serve!

These three prophecies were then given to us:

> 'Spring Valley is a mission station in the jungle of wealth and not like missions in the remote jungles of the world. It therefore calls for different priorities.'

> 'Spring Valley must be planned so that the necessary work can be done with the minimum of effort, time and waste, so that time and energy can be available for God's work.'

> 'God's economy is never cheap – there's a difference between doing something for a little money and doing something cheaply.'

Not only were the spiritual foundations being laid, but the foundations for the stables were also completed. This was with the regular help of our friends who were helping us so much in 'obedience to the Lord', as they put it. We then moved on to bricking up to damp course level. We thanked God when permission was granted at this point for a further five horses.

Schools began to express interest in booking in, but we were waiting until we acquired a minibus. We had built up to having forty pupils a week, but we could not build up any further until we found adequate transport. We managed to borrow a minibus from the church. The children were so encouraged that the Lord loved them so much that He supplied the transport for them to come horse riding.

March 1986

The Lord does all things well. Often it is in discovering His plan that everything then simply falls into place. For instance, we were in need of two glass doors for the stable office. Our neighbour said, 'Come and look at mine.'

We went, and they were very different from what we had in mind. They were enormous doors complete with huge brass handles. 'I don't know,' I hesitated, 'but let's see if they will fit.'

The doors fitted perfectly, and once we got used to the idea, we realized that they were far better than what we had had in mind, as well as far stronger, with thick safety glass.

The Lord then provided us with a very presentable red and white minibus. Here He moved by closing and opening the right doors until we discovered the one we believed He had in mind for us. This we bought at a very reasonable price. The miracle was that, because we were building the stables at a third of the price we thought it would cost, we had sufficient money left over to buy the minibus. Now we could collect children from the schools.

We were quite overwhelmed by all the Lord was doing. A couple of ladies from our church felt called to give us a meal on the very busy days. This was difficult to accept, but who are we to reject what the Lord has given? One day we were given a large dish of food. The next day the Lord sent a lot of extra hands to help with the building. We were all very busy and came in hungry at 1.00 pm. We opened the fridge to this large glass dish of food. It was enough to feed all twelve of us. This gave us time for prayer before the afternoon began, and to thank the Lord yet again for supplying every need.

We also had a need for whitewash, the powder type which was off the market. A friend 'phoned to say a friend of hers was cleaning out a warehouse. She was about to throw away thirty boxes of old powder white wash. It was given to us!

We proved too that the Lord gives the very best. A need arose for a horse to accompany rides, and with which to teach and demonstrate. We placed this need in the Lord's hands in prayer, and agreed to accept the Lord's decision on a horse, well prepared to carry on without one. It was the very next day that the 'phone rang. Four horses were about to be put down unless someone could give them a home that very day. My friend Marina and I raced to the track. She received the very quiet horse she was looking for; and I was led to see the unbroken colt. They opened the door to one of the most beautiful horses I have ever seen. The horse Prihat Aviv arrived within an hour by horsebox. I soon managed to get him used to a saddle on his back and mounted him. He was just what I had always wanted. I kept running to his stable. Was it really true? He was really there. I praised and thanked God!

April 1986

Isaiah 55:9 says:

> 'For as the heavens are higher than the earth, so are my ways higher than your ways, and my thoughts than your thoughts.'
>
> (KJV)

This also appeared to apply to Spring Valley. We had a very dangerous road in to Spring Valley. Getting out up the steep road caused many problems, necessitating the use of first gear three or four times, and there was no way of seeing if a car was coming. Consequently, in order to emerge from the entrance on your departure, customers would not be able to see what traffic was coming before they pulled out. It was a risky manoeuvre even though it was not a busy road.

'Let's fill in the pot-holes, maybe with some cement strips,' I suggested. However, the Lord had a different solution, and, as if He did not speak clearly enough, a bulldozer was at work on the next door farm and He supplied a friend who had designed a new road with a more gradual incline.

*The local council lays the new entrance into
Spring Valley free of charge*

*Riding School pupils line up in front
of the new stables*

The bulldozer arrived, and within the day, the new road was built, complete with a car park. At the same time, he also levelled the ground for the next Christian Camp Site buildings, which were our next project.

The next step was how to gravel the road. A week had almost passed, and no-one could supply gravel for at least a month. We made alternative arrangements for a delivery of ash. It did not arrive because of a strike. Eventually I felt the Lord tell me to cancel it, so I obeyed. On Monday, at 2.20 pm, hearing lots of noise, I ran up to see a large truck unloading gravel. It was from the local Council. They said that, as it was the entrance only, they had decided to do it free of charge.

The Lord's thoughts are much bigger than our little ones, and when He moves, He certainly moves. The Lord had been at work in ways I had least expected, for the picture in my thinking and the work that the Lord was engaged in, were entirely different.

> *'What is man, that You are mindful of him?'* (Psalm 8:4)

The reality of this humbles one so. God is at work, and we can never deserve it. Such great love transcends all, and in tears of joy we are able to respond to God.

The Lord continued His work. He supplied us with (amongst other things) a new Welsh pony that the children named 'Elli Shever', meaning 'God's gift'. We also had a successful holiday camp where the children grew spiritually. The Riding School became established with ten horses and fifty pupils per week. It was all due to the Lord. With the stables nearly completed, we felt that we could now begin to concentrate on the Christian Centre.

Here again, the **Lord had known our need ahead of us**. We really had to step out in faith as to how to finance it. We decided to sell our cows, and raised the equivalent of £750 from them towards the Hall. Then the Lord miraculously supplied a further £1,000 towards the project.

Some Questions to Think About

- How can you reach out to people in your area?
- What are the giftings that the Lord has given to you?
- What do you think is to be your Jerusalem?
- How will you go about making your Jerusalem a reality?

Spring Valley Holiday Farm – My Judea

March 1987

> 'Crimson clouds slip behind the hills closing yet another day at Spring Valley. The ha-di-dahs, two by two, swoop noisily down onto the trees, while hundreds of smaller birds fly gaily through the sweet evening air. So much beauty out here, in hill and dale, one day to share with others.'

So reads an entry from my March 1987 diary entry for Spring Valley.

Yet the day was arriving fast, the plans were through and the foundations were marked out. On the Monday, Wilfrid would begin digging the foundations for the Hall.

During the holidays, we held five Camps where a few children made decisions for Christ, then they went back to school and lessons were back to normal.

Wilfrid had built and completed the cottage for our farm workers and they had moved in.

But it has not all just been plain sailing. The building plans for the holiday farm, for instance, were deferred four times until we decided to pray and fast on the day of the next planners' meeting – and they were passed that day.

Also with every victory, we tended to get faced with spiritual warfare, a thing with which both Wilfrid and I had had practically no experience. We asked for prayers regarding this, for it was not very pleasant. Yes, we knew that God was stronger and with tears of determination, we called on His name, awaiting victory.

This proved that God truly answers prayer, and brings the impossible into reality as we rely totally on Him.

The foundations for the Christian Centre were then completed and were passed by the inspectors. We were now ready to build, and we prayed for the windows, doors and beams. How the windows arrived was a special miracle.

I had a 'phone call and the man said, 'I have a strange question to ask you. Are you building something for the Lord?'

'Yes, we are building a Christian Holiday Farm.'

'That is the confirmation I was looking for', he answered. 'I will send you some windows within the week because the Lord has told me to give them to you, I just needed confirmation first.'

I thanked him joyfully and within a week, the windows arrived.

The beams were next – supplied through a member of our congregation – plus poles to complete the fencing through yet another parishioner. Only the Lord could have told them, for we did not utter a word of our need. We then waited to see how the Lord would supply the doors.

Yes, we are commanded to live by faith. We knew it was an impossibility to build the Centre without money, yet we knew we must walk in faith and expectancy, serving our great and mighty God.

May 1987

The Christian Centre was now halfway up with Wilfrid in charge. That is to say, the hall, kitchen, lounge and washing block. We decided to complete this half before commencing the rooms. The Lord had complete control of our building operations. He brought to us the right workers, and supplied the materials we needed.

Marius and Frankie du Preez joined us in the beginning of March. They came to see our cottage and moved in that very day. They then began to work with us and trusted the Lord with us day by day.

We were all amateur builders and therefore had to look to the Lord for everything – how to do it, where to use the materials the Lord gave us, in the way He would want them used.

For instance, we were given a pile of windows – 'Which windows are for where?' we asked. We knew that the Lord always supplies exactly what we need. 'It's easy then, if we need four small windows for the washing block and two for the kitchen, then there must be six in the pile.' We sorted them out, and sure enough, there were exactly six of them!

We carried on building. The Lord was the Foreman. Our job was to simply discover what He wanted from us and then to obey. The results? The building grew!

It was an amazing experience to serve the Lord in this way. He is so exact, even to the smallest details, so much so that we were able to carry on building with a bank balance equivalent to around £200, completely worry-free. We knew that there too, He would supply the exact amount needed, providing that we stayed in His will.

We recognised that people were praying for us and that miracles were happening. We thanked the Lord for all that He was doing. He is wonderful.

July 1987

'Stay in an attitude of prayer and faith and I will do the rest', said the Lord.

That month we had a lot to pray about. We were unable to find any second-hand roofing and were running out of money. We needed purloins and rafters to hold the roofing up, and we needed ceiling boards. We needed scaffolding to erect the gables and we needed to find a cheap way of flooring the centre. Apart from the centre, we needed to do something about the fact that our horses were over-grazing Spring Valley. We also needed help with the very full Saturday riding lessons.

We prayed about all of this, and then left it in the Lord's hands, not knowing where to start or how so many needs could possibly be met, or how they could ever be financed.

We then gasped in amazement as the Lord answered each prayer one after another, without further action on our part.

Firstly, we had a cheque for the equivalent of £200 from the Diocese of Port Elizabeth and then a further £200 from All Saints' Church. Next, we had a 'phone call from the Newton Park Baptist Church: 'We want to donate £2,000 towards a new roof for the Hall and then send our "mission outreach house church" to help erect it.' It was very hard to believe my ears at this very unexpected phone call. 'The Lord has spoken to us,' he assured us, 'and we believe He wants a new roof on His Centre. Will you please get us the best quote so that we can make out the cheque.' After some phone calls we got a quote for the equivalent of £3,000 for new roofing for the entire Centre. We believed we could raise the other £1,000 from our account along with the gifts.

I phoned Shalom Woodworks and the owner donated the purloins as well as giving us the ceiling boards at cost price – another fantastic surprise. Next, Hans Jorritsma, who had helped with our stables, arrived with scaffolding and cement slabs for the outside walk-way of the rooms. He had also experimented on an ash flooring at half the price of a cement one, with success.

The Lord even solved our grazing problems by enabling us to rent the whole of the next-door farm at £50 a month. Not only was there excellent grazing, but the most beautiful walks through rivers and forest. The owner also had an Olympic-sized swimming pool that he said he would prepare for the campers to use that coming summer. Even Saturday help was arranged from amongst the clients. Every single prayer was answered within that month!

The building had progressed and preparations were made for the roofing of the kitchen, prayer room and hall.

It was both exciting and awesome to see the Lord at work in this way – supplying every need and answering every prayer. Somehow, in my spirit, I could sense that there was more to this than the eye could see.

We were seeing the Lord at work and it was not for nothing. I believed that He was making preparations for revival, and I believed that He was preparing us. I desired that we and the church would hear Him and respond, that we would wake up out of our slumber and see that the Lord was amongst us.

August 1987

A Roof Wetting Celebration of Praise and Thanksgiving was planned in the newly roofed Hall at Spring Valley Christian Centre on Sunday the 9th August at 3.00 pm. Christians from various different churches were invited and we had a good turnout.

The roofing had arrived and we were busy erecting it. We were not finished yet though. We still had the floors to do, plastering, painting, woodwork, electricity and plumbing. Yet the first big milestone had been reached. The roofing was certainly a reason for praise and thanksgiving to God.

It is the Lord indeed who did all this. We started out in faith with the equivalent of about £20 and we still had £20. Sometimes though, we did get weak. How would we pay the wages this week? How could we order grit for flooring without the money to pay for it? There were two alternatives. One was to panic, the other was to look up to God again, pray and ask for our needs to be met. Then trust and wait. Over and over again the needs were supplied, sometimes even at the last moment. Our labourers were always paid on time and the urgent needs always met. Yet we still had many needs for the completion of the Centre. However, we knew we could still trust God.

One day I actually had to tell our labourers that I had no money to pay them their 300 Rands with. I went to my Riding Lesson diary to take the 45 Rands I had just earned through teaching riding, when I saw an envelope with my name on it. I opened it and to my amazement found exactly 300 Rands inside it, just enough to pay the labourers. I have no idea how it got there, only God knows.

Due to this miracle, one of these workers phoned me from Johannesburg a year later saying, 'Remember the day when God supplied our wages in that envelope?'

'Yes,' I replied.

'Well, I've never forgotten it,' he went on, 'and last night, because of that miracle, I accepted Jesus as my Lord and Saviour. I just had to phone you this morning to let you know.'

Our minibus broke down; it was only a disconnected wire. It had to be connected up if the car was to be driven. We asked for prayer that we would remain 'connected up' with the Lord, that He might use us in the way He wished and that we would respond to Him, even as a car that is driven by the owner.

Just when, for the first time since the work began, work was grinding to a halt due to the funds supply drying up, we received the equivalent of £450 in Rands. Praise the Lord! This was at just the right time! And a 150 Rand reimbursement, which covered the costs of going to the Rhulani Refugee Camp, enabled us to carry on with the building. We again asked our supporters to thank the Lord with us for supplying our needs yet again.

Soon the Spring Valley Holiday Farm and Riding Centre were established and the Charismatic Revival filled us up with campers every weekend. God blessed us in many ways and we had the joy of leading many to Christ. We also built ourselves a house after this and the Prinsloo family who had already helped us every weekend with the riding school (and Martin Prinsloo had built all our show jumps) also helped us build our house. One day, while erecting the roof of our house, Martin trod on a sheet of loose roofing, which slipped off the double storey building and fell all

The opening of Spring Valley, 29th November 1987

Spring Valley:
campers having fun on our lake

the way to the ground with him on top of it. However, the piece of roofing appeared to glide down like a parachute and he was unharmed except for a sore heal. We all thanked the Lord for His protection.

We thought that we were now settled for life, yet this was just the beginning.

Some Questions to Think About

- What miracles has God already done in your life?
- In what ways do you need to trust God to supply?
- How can you stay connected up with the Lord?
- Are you ready to step out in faith now?

Standlake Equestrian Centre & Ranch – My Samaria

1996

It was seven years later that the Lord gave us a burden for the youth in England and it did not go away, so in 1992 I flew over to England to try and find out what the Lord wanted us to do about it. By this time Rebecca, our daughter, was two years old. She was born in 1990, seven years after we got married. We named her Rebecca because of the two seven-year periods that Wilfrid had waited.

I phoned Christian Camping International and they put me in touch with the Fairglade Trust who were going to buy twenty-five acres, to start a Youth Camp. They actually offered us the job of setting up the riding school side once they had bought the land. They showed me a very overgrown, undeveloped piece of land and my first thoughts were, 'Oh no, too much work needed here,' and I flew back to South Africa, rather disappointed and told Wilfrid about it. Wilfrid advised we prayed more about it, for he wanted, beyond all things, to be in the centre of God's will.

Yet the burden would not lift, so in desperation we laid out a fleece before the Lord, saying, 'If you want us in England, then show us by a phone call from England to offer us a short-term job. If we get no 'phone call then we know to stay here at our established and very successful Spring Valley.' We did not expect anything more. The next day, we did not get one phone call offering us jobs in England, but two! Only God could have done that and we knew we had to obey. So, within three weeks, in September 1993, we were ready to go to England.

Within the three weeks Spring Valley was rented out as we accepted the first job in Loughborough. I kept the phone number of the second job, just in case.

We arrived in Leicester to a small upstairs flat and had to start work at 8.00 am after caring for my two-year-old daughter, Rebecca. Often I had to teach riding until after 9.00 pm. I found the job hard after running my own riding schools for so many years.

Four months passed and I was able to take Christmas leave to attend a teaching clinic in the USA. In the USA I met many people who ran Christian camps with horse programmes so I showed them the book 'The Biblical Approach to Horsemanship' that the Lord had enabled me to write. They loved it and bought hundreds of copies from me. I was also invited to run clinics at Faith Ranch, Ohio. When I returned I was in trouble for having witnessed to a lady going through a divorce. The groom had overheard me and had told my boss. I was told that I was not to witness for Jesus on their yard. I replied that I was unable to agree and unless they allowed me to share my faith with others, I would have to give a month's notice. They accepted the month's notice.

Next day we took the train to meet with the people who had made the second phone call that we had received in South Africa. By the evening we had signed a two-year contract with them to start a Christian riding school for the Christian Campsite across the road and to train up a local girl to British Riding Instructor qualifications to run it, once we left. The next two years were happy as we worked for good people, but selling Spring Valley was very hard. On Good Friday 1995 I signed the contract of sale at a very reduced price for Christian buyers, giving it up to follow Christ. We found out later that God honoured our obedience, but at the time it was very difficult.

Then the Rand went from R5 to the pound to R10 to the pound, not helping either. We also gave the money that others had given to us back to them to help with other projects. How could we ever go ahead now? Our only hope was the Fairglade Trust who had offered us the job of opening up a riding school on the land they were buying in Standlake, Oxfordshire.

Then one month from the end of our contract we got a letter stating that they were no longer buying the land. We were devastated. We had given up Spring Valley to serve the Lord in England and so far were effectively not doing so.

'Lord,' I called out crying, 'Why are they not buying the Standlake land?'

And the Lord quietly replied, 'Because you are buying it.'

'**What**? We don't have enough money to buy land in England.'

'Yes, you do.'

I phoned the Fairglade Trust immediately.

'We have not bought the land because five acres have been bought for a travellers' camp, leaving only twenty acres.'

'How much is the land?' I enquired. I discovered it was much cheaper than I expected, only £3,000 less than what we had. The very next day, I went to see the land and paid a deposit. They gave us a month to find the balance.

We bought a £300 mobile home and hired a digger to make a road through the hedge on to the property so we could get the mobile home onto it. At the same time, they dredged part of the lake of dangerous sinking clay and willow trees for water for us and our three horses and cleared three acres in front for paddocks. We moved in on 1st March 1996.

I phoned my mother to come over from South Africa with some money from the sale of Spring Valley. She was allowed to bring £5,000. This paid off the balance on the land and enabled us to build two stables and a feed room. It also bought a horsebox and a pony called Kerry. Now, we could open a riding school to earn a living, and one day build a Christian Holiday Ranch.

I took the £8.50 balance to open an account at the bank and

also was hoping to borrow £5,000 to set up the riding school, but they said, 'No job, no house, no money; a bad proposition, sorry.'

What could I do? I left the £8.50 for a rainy day and told them, 'We will trust God, then.'

That was the best decision we ever made, for God has blessed in every way ever since, and it would take a full book to share all that God did.

Our three horses soon became four, then five, until we had up to eight pupils a class and around a hundred pupils a week. Then the balance of the Spring Valley money arrived, which built the indoor school. Within a year we had gone from breaking the ice, that first very cold March to bucket water to the three horses and mobile home, to getting a pump, sanitation and electricity; and now the indoor school.

In 1997 I was driving to Witney when the Lord suddenly said, 'Drive to Eynsham' (a small town about six miles away from Witney). Did I hear right? 'Drive to Eynsham,' He insisted.

'Eynsham? Why? What for?' I asked.

'Drive to Eynsham.'

So I turned round and drove to Eynsham.

As I arrived, I saw they were demolishing an office block, so drove in to see if I could buy something towards the Holiday Ranch one day. I bought a First-Aid Box for the riding school.

'Surely the Lord did not get me here to buy a First-Aid Box?' I thought. I looked around. Those Cotswold stones are nice, but they would be far too expensive for us to buy, I thought. I decided to ask.

'Oh those, we've had no offer for those. Look, you can have the lot for the price of the delivery, if you can take the lot.'

'I'll take the lot,' I replied.

Sixteen loads of Cotswold stone therefore cost us £100 per load! This was of God. After three years we were allowed to build ourselves a house, which a local farmer helped us with. As we had no builder, it cost way below the normal price to build. What a pleasure it was to move into our own house. By this time, the riding school had sixteen stables and we thought it would be nice to have an outdoor arena.

'Lord, we have the money for the digger, but not the sand. If You supply the sand somehow, then we will know You want us to have one.'

Three days later we were offered eight loads of sand, so we hired the digger.

Halfway through levelling the land, the digger man called me. 'You can't put sand on this clay,' he said. 'It will sink right through. You need at least sixteen loads of gravel first.'

'That is a problem,' I replied. 'Lord,' I prayed, 'What do we do now?'

'Follow Me!' I felt the leading to walk to the edge of the arena.

'Come,' I called to the driver. I walked outside the arena and felt led to stop.

'Dig here and you shall find some,' I felt the Lord say.

'The Lord says, "Dig here and you shall find some."'

'Come on,' said the driver, 'there's no gravel down there!'

'Yes, there is!' I replied.

'No way!' he said.

'Please dig, you will find it.'

'Never,' he replied.

'Please just dig.'

'Look,' said the driver, 'I will dig to prove you wrong.'

'Thank you!'

He dug down about three feet and found beautiful red gravel just perfect for the job! I left him to do it, thanking God for showing us. Later that day the digger man called me again. The gravel had run out and it only did the first half of the arena. Then, with a smile across his face, he said, 'Seeing that your God supplied gravel for the first half of the arena, let's see if He can also supply gravel for the other half!'

'No problem,' I replied and whispered, 'Lord, where is it?' and I walked to the other end.

'Bank' came into my mind, so I called out, 'The bank. The

gravel is in the bank.' And, sure enough, there it was, enough to finish off the entire arena and at the same time discover the original entrance to the property.

The next problem was how to get eight lorry-loads of sand across the muddy field. Just then his mobile rang. He had a new job of moving sixteen tons of stone from Witney and dumping it. He looked at me and said, 'If I can dump that stone between your driveway and the arena, I will build you a road to the arena, free of charge from what I save on dumping fees.'

'Done,' I replied.

This was how God provided us with a lovely road to the arena. This road has been a real asset to the horses and riders too.

Soon the road was built and they drove the lorries of sand onto the arena. Then a traveller from next door offered us some wood as kicking boards at a very reasonable price. A beautiful well-built Olympic-sized arena, which should have cost about £15,000, cost only £1,000! That's God!

All this time we were trying to save up money to build the Holiday Ranch at the cheapest price and we gave up more than once. I discovered that a steel frame and wood was the cheapest way to build, but the Lord, I felt, wanted a forty-bed triple-storey and my faith just could not reach that far. After all, even a thirty-bed ranch was out of our reach. Even that could take a lifetime to build. So being practical, I put in plans for a thirty-bed ranch and the plans were passed.

I then ordered the double-storey steel frame and they came to erect it. As I looked up I saw instead a triple-storey steel frame with a much steeper roof than I had ordered, as well as higher sides. I phoned them up and they were not even aware of it.

'So, if the Lord has somehow delivered to us a triple-storey building at the price of a double-storey,' I thought to myself, 'He must mean He wants a forty-bed campsite, not a thirty-bed campsite!'

I went back to the planners. They agreed to the extra storey. Then the building regulations were also passed, and then there was to be a steel test to see if the steel could hold an extra storey.

It passed the steel test. Only one more miracle to go, and the Lord did that as well. The money came in and all three storeys were completed at once. I only had faith for a thirty-bed campsite, yet the Lord still did it. The forty-bed, three-storey building was completed, without borrowing money, no mortgage at all. Only God can do that, and all three storeys have been booked up, weekend after weekend, ever since.

There were so many more miracles; all our furniture was given; all the conference chairs were given. A local supermarket was putting in a new restaurant, so I wrote and asked them what they intended to do with the old chairs, as we would like to purchase them for our Youth Camp.

A lovely letter came back. 'Come on 28th of this month and you can have them all.'

We collected eight round tables and forty wicker chairs with pink cushion seats; all top quality and strong and we scrubbed them up like new.

Bunk beds and mattresses were also given, but we only had a few odd sheets and I put them on and had to go and collect Rebecca from school. When I got back, Wilfrid said, 'Someone has given these black sacks full of something for the Centre.' I opened them to find matching bottom sheets and pillowcases. I put them straight on. Light-blue for two dormitories, dark-blue for two dormitories and wine red for the top storey. Exactly enough! That's God.

And so the ranch opened and there was not even time to advertise as almost every weekend was being booked up with campers through word of mouth. That's God!

Meanwhile the Lord was doing something new in my life again. He asked me to go on a conference on a Saturday.

'Lord, you know I can't do that on a Saturday, that's our main income.'

'Who do you put first?' He asked.

'You, Lord.'

'I'm afraid not, if you are staying to teach. Employ someone else to teach on a Saturday and go to the conference.'

I obeyed and went. It was hard at first to employ someone else to do my work, but things went well and then the Lord told me to employ this person to teach full-time, for He had a new job for me.

Some Questions to Think About

- When God leads us by a burden that will not lift, we must obey Him; what does this mean to you?
- Difficult times may come to sift us and cause us to grow in Christ. This is when we need to trust Him entirely and not give up. Think of how difficult times have helped you get closer to God.
- How does this chapter challenge you? What do you feel you could do about it?

New miracle arena complete

To the Ends of the Earth

I went to the meeting in Oxford to listen to an evangelist called David Hathaway from Eurovision. This man spoke with authority. He really loved God and challenged us greatly. I bought his book *Why Siberia?* and practically prayed my way through it. I wanted to live just like that for God and had had a dream of myself being in Russia as an evangelist, so I wrote to David and he answered my letter. I then received his magazine, *Prophetic Vision* through the post.

He was taking a group to Israel and I desperately wanted to go, but really, even though I wanted to serve God as an evangelist like him, I was only Suzanne, a riding teacher, and a girl at that, with a family. Who did I think I was anyway? Surely not worthy enough to serve God this way? I had tried for years and was always told to sit down.

David was speaking again in Northampton so I decided to go and hear him speak and give him the money to send anyone he wished to Israel. This I did. He took the money and pointing straight at me said, 'You need to be in Jerusalem,' and he sent me the ticket to go. So I went.

In Jerusalem we were having communion at the Garden Tomb when the Lord spoke to me and said, 'Abide in Me and I will abide in you and will go with you wherever I shall send you.' This caused me to cry with joy.

'Fire Over Jerusalem Conference':
the day I heard God's voice at the Garden Tomb

'Fire Over Kenya Conference':
speaking and praying for the sick

Bala Orphanage: praying for the orphans
(the orphanage now has over 300 orphans)

'Fire Over Kenya Conference': Margaret, the wife of a witch-doctor,
blind for seven years, now can see

The next day I was invited to Kenya. I accepted but at the last minute the team leader could not go, causing me to have to step into his shoes as main speaker and pray for the sick.

When I arrived I was told that **people were walking four days to receive their healing**! (As I indicated earlier in this book, this really struck me.) Now I really got worried and realized I needed to pray for my life.

I cried out to God at a level I had not up to then experienced, 'Please, Lord help. I can give these people nothing, only You can help them.'

After thirty minutes of crying I heard His voice and felt His peace. 'If I can cry through your eyes like this, I can also heal through your hands like this.'

That night I spoke to about 300 people, called for salvation and then had to step out in faith. 'Anyone sick?'

Thirty rushed forward. The first three were totally blind.

'Lord!' I called out, then I remembered it was Reinhardt Bonnke's first healing in the power of the Holy Spirit, *also* when the man of God never turned up. He simply said, 'In Jesus' name, blind eyes open,' and they were healed.

It seemed OK to use the same words, so I said, almost in Reinhardt's German accent, 'In the name of Jesus, blind eyes open.'

'I can see,' came the answer.

'What!' I replied.

'I can see!'

'Can you really see?'

'Yes, I can really see.'

'Go and testify,' I told her and went to the second person, who was also instantly healed and then the third also could suddenly see. The fourth with malaria was healed in a minute, then somebody with a paralysed arm. All thirty people received their healing that night, plus another 240 through the next three days.

I came home to England and doors just opened everywhere. Before I knew it, I was travelling overseas on a regular basis.

In Malawi, I saw the Lord heal three children out of wheelchairs. In Nigeria, I watched Jesus heal a lady who suffered with a paralysed right side and could not speak for twenty years following her stroke. The Lord healed her in exactly $2\frac{1}{2}$ minutes, which I still have on video.

In Latvia, a lady came for prayer who suffered greatly with arthritis. Her knees would not function properly at all. After I had prayed for her she went to the ladies' cloakroom. She returned, full of joy saying, 'I can get up without help!' She told everyone.

In Ghana, I watched the Lord heal a lady from severe arthritis in a couple of minutes, enabling her to walk.

In Kenya, an elderly lady with polio had been unable to stand or use her left arm and leg for many years. I prayed for the arm first and suddenly she was able to move it. She then got up and walked, completely healed.

In Italy, a lady with a paralysed arm for twenty years was suddenly healed and she was so excited that she went off to cut grapes with it.

Back in Latvia I saw a recreation miracle. A sixteen-year-old girl was born with a crooked jaw from birth. As I prayed, I saw nothing happen. That night, as I told the pastor that three had not received their healing suddenly, she ran up and said, 'Look at my jaw, look at my teeth.' We all burst into tears with joy and gratitude to the Lord. She looked so pretty with a straight jaw and normal teeth.

In South Africa, I saw a girl who had never walked, because of a twisted spine, walk with a walker within half an hour. Three months later she did not even need a walking stick. In Mozambique, I saw two deaf and dumb instantly healed, and in Uganda three or four hundred healed within two minutes. The blind saw, the deaf heard and the lame leapt up and walked. That was the most powerful demonstration of the Lord's healing power I've seen. Other countries then opened up and I found myself speaking in Bulgaria, Romania, the Philippines, India, Pakistan and the USA.

*Pelesia Awiao, unable to use her left arm and leg for many years
due to polio, suddenly gets up and walks after prayer*

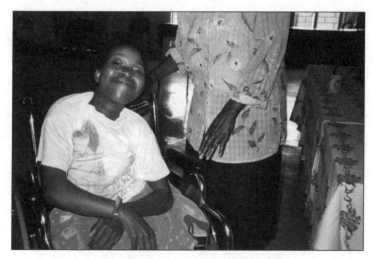

*Maria Ekoneane: born with a twisted spine,
she had never been able to stand for seventeen years*

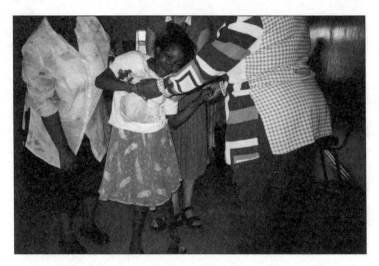

Maria: after prayer she stands for the first time in her life

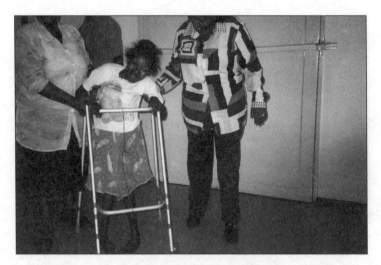

Maria: walking with the aid of a walker within half an hour – after three months she can walk unaided after complete healing by the Lord

These are just a few healings that I remember out of many, many more. It is worth noting that the orphans in Bala Orphanage, which we opened in Kenya in 2001, have such a simple faith in God that when they are sick they are instantly healed by praying to be healed in Jesus' name.

Yet God was doing even more than healing. He heals because He has compassion. He also heals to show that He alone is God and there is no other. He is our never-changing God, the God who led the Israelites out of Egypt and led them to the Promised Land, the God who spoke through the prophets, the God who sent His only Son Jesus to die on the cross and rise on the third day to set us free. Right to this very day, He moves in power and might. He moves in ways that make us marvel.

It is not for us to decide what we wish to do for God, but rather to see what the Father is doing. When we begin to see what the Father is doing and how He wants us to do it, then something far greater than one could ever think or imagine happens. Every ministry is unique; one cannot copy another, but only do what the Father has commanded.

In Uganda the Lord said, 'I want you to reach every village.'

'That's impossible,' I replied 'it would take me two lifetimes just to reach every village in Uganda.'

'I will show you how,' came the reply.

Within a week the Lord raised up thirty evangelists for Kenya and twenty for Uganda. There was only one problem. How could they get there? If only they had a bicycle and maybe a megaphone with which to call the people together.

So I came home to England and people gave money for bicycles and soon we had twenty evangelists with bicycles, megaphones and Bibles. With these twenty bicycles, these evangelists visited 300 villages, planted thirty-five churches and twenty preaching points by the end of the year.

Now came another problem. How could they train up new pastors and evangelists to look after the newly planted churches? All the Bible Schools were too expensive. The people are poor.

Well, I sent them teaching letters every six weeks and I thought that that was all I could do.

God had another plan. I went into the Philippines to do evangelism. This had been arranged through a wise, elderly man called Bishop Blanco. 'Sit down,' he invited. I sat down. He looked across the table at me seriously. He said, 'God has been giving me courses for a Bible School for over thirty years.' He said that these Bible Courses are going to become an International Bible School. God told me to give this Bible School to a certain person. 'This morning,' he continued, 'I heard the Lord say I was to give them to you, for you are going to set up an International Bible School.'

I was stunned. I said nothing. I mean, who was I? I then asked the Lord what He thought about all this and the Lord immediately answered, 'All is in place and ready for it.' I suddenly realized this was true. Eurovision had given me the African contacts to follow up, but postage was proving too expensive, so instead I gave all the contacts of each country to the lead pastor in charge to post the teaching letters to them at local postal costs and the lead pastor not only sent on the teaching letters, but also visited them. He networked them with all the denominations of churches into the different areas of the country to help with village evangelism.

Regardless of how I felt about it all, I knew that Bishop Blanco had the answer to the training of all these evangelists and pastors the Lord was raising up and that this Bible School would be free of charge. So I gratefully received these valuable well-written Bible Courses to be handed on to many.

By January 2006, we had sent the notes for the Bible School first semester to Malawi, Mozambique, Kenya, Uganda, Ghana, Togo, Liberia and Nigeria. By March, the Bible School had got into Pakistan and had been translated into Urdu. By May, Ghana had 200 students, and by July the Bible School had been planted in all ten regions of the country, with about 500 students waiting to start. Even many friends in England wanted to do it so I ended

Step Out in Faith Bible School, Delta Region, Ghana

Babe: healed from arthritic knees and elbows, now able to walk without crutches. Bishop Blanco, founder of Step Out in Faith Bible School holds up her crutches

up having classes every Wednesday evening in our newly constructed Prayer House (Wilfrid and others had built this prayer room with some of the remaining stones from the 1997 visit to Eynsham).

God does all things well and He wants us to complete the Great Commission. People also gave towards more bicycles and by April we were able to send money for a further forty-seven bicycles, megaphones and Bibles.

God has done it all. He is equipping the pastors with His Word. He is supplying the bicycles to get to the villages and on top of that He has caused revival to break out in the villages. Sometimes entire villages come to Christ with a single visit. One Pastor from Mozambique writes and says, 'The bicycle ministry is working so very well. The gospel of Jesus is spreading through the villages like a bush fire.'

Yes, this is the power of the gospel. This is the power of the written Word of God. The book of Revelation describes God's voice as being like thunder coming forth, with the power of lightning; God's Word from God's mouth, His 'Yes' from His mouth so that we can trust it. God lives outside the realm of time. His spoken Word is alive and active and His written Word, our Bible, is also as alive and active. If we know that God's answer is 'Yes', we can praise Him even before it happens, because we know that in the spiritual realm it is already done, even as in Acts 16:25–26:

> 'About midnight Paul and Silas were praying and singing hymns to God, and the other prisoners were listening to them. Suddenly there was such a violent earthquake that the foundations of the prison were shaken. At once all the prison doors flew open, and everybody's chains came loose.'   (NIV)

They praised God before they were released and suddenly their chains fell off and they were free. This is the faith God is looking for. Even in the building of two holiday camps, I have seen this is true, as I saw the completed holiday camp even before it was built. Even though we had no money we knew God wanted these holiday camps built so we could go on faith, knowing God would do it and He did do it, without borrowing money and without a mortgage. If we can trust Him in the physical realm, then we can also trust Him for healings and victory over all evil.

The written Word of God, our Bible, is as powerful as God's Word in God's mouth. When we speak God's Word, when we speak the written Word, by the authority of the powerful name of Jesus, something wonderful happens through the power of the Holy Spirit. His Word in your mouth becomes as powerful as His Word in His mouth and it is done. As you train up other local evangelists to spread the Word something wonderful happens in their lives too. As they speak God's Word to the people in the authority of the name of Jesus and in the power of the Holy Spirit, their words become as powerful; people are set free, delivered and healed.

When people see these wonderful healings that only Jesus can do, then the word goes out and hundreds come, not only to receive their healings, but to receive this glorious Jesus who loves us so much that He died on the Cross to break the power of sin and death and then He rose from the dead in complete victory over every evil thing.

It is through His love that we are set free from the Evil One. It is by His love that He forgives our sin and gives us eternal life. It is through His love that we are healed; and it is by His redemptive love that He gives us eternal life. All these gifts can be ours, simply by our acknowledging that we are sinners and asking for His forgiveness.

Some Questions to Think About

- Where do you need to trust God?
- Are you prepared to step out in faith in the area that God has prepared for you?
- How do you find God's blueprint for your ministry?
- When do you need to start?

Beggar healed in Jesus' name: after suffering a stroke a year ago and being paralysed on his right side, he gets up and walks

Walking with God and Village Revival

The Lord is not just interested in reaching a few, He is interested in reaching whole villages, cities, countries and nations and if we are obedient, He can use mere human beings just like you and me to do it. When we obey God, even when we don't know what we are doing, God is able to do far more through us than we can ever think or imagine.

Nigeria

In 2004 in Nigeria we had a crusade cancelled due to some emergency. Now I had two days with nothing to do so I asked the pastor to arrange that I speak anywhere, prisons, schools, just anywhere.

He arranged that I speak in a prison. That very day seventy people accepted Christ and at a High School the next morning over 200 pupils responded to Jesus and some of the children and teachers also received healing. As we were leaving a TV crew arrived to film the children breaking up for their holidays and we drove back to where I was staying. Suddenly the Lord said, 'Turn round and go to the TV studio.' Was I hearing right? What would we go there for? I mentioned this to the driver and we thought that maybe we should return to the school where we saw the TV crew arriving. So we returned to the school, but the

TV crew had already left. Confused, I prayed again. 'The TV studios.' So we went to the TV studios and walked aimlessly in.

Not knowing what we had come for, we decided to ask for the religious department and found it. We told the lady what we were doing in Nigeria and she said, 'You need to see the special editions manager. Come back at 4.00 pm. He will be here then.'

We went back to the house and as we were about to return to the TV studios the Lord said, 'Take your TV broadcast VHS tape with you.' So I did.

We arrived in good time, knocked on the manager's door and walked in and shook hands. Not knowing quite what to say, I handed him the VHS tape and he immediately put it on and watched it. After about ten minutes he looked up and said, 'I like this. Can you come here 8.00 am tomorrow? I would like to interview you live for thirty minutes and then I want to do another programme on you after that.'

That was it. God had done it and two broadcasts with the gospel, prayer of salvation and prayer for the sick, went out nationwide to reach millions at no cost to ourselves. God thinks big. He allowed the crusade of several hundred people to be cancelled in order that I could speak to millions through the two TV programmes.

Malawi

Later that year I had a similar experience in Malawi. It was a day on which I had nothing planned. I was thinking of going up to the waterfall in the Maluzi mountains when I thought I should ask what the Lord had in mind. 'Go to the radio station, then the TV broadcast, and then buy five bicycles and megaphones,' seemed to come to me.

I then asked Pastor James Undi, our organiser, 'Is there a radio station in Blantyre?'

'Yes, come I will show you.'

We caught a mini-bus, crossed the road and went straight in.

'Have you come to speak on radio?' someone asked us.

'Yes, sure, if you want us to!'

Apparently we had arrived just in time to fill a thirty-minute space, which had just become vacant. We were interviewed as to why we had come to Blantyre and we also gave the gospel message and invited people to pray the sinner's prayer.

'Can you do devotions?' I was asked.

'Why not?' I replied. 'What on?'

'You tell me, just five-minute slots though.' I think.

'Is the Lord's Prayer suitable?' I asked.

'Five slots or ten slots?'

'Make it ten', I answered.

I sat down; I was given the microphone. A silent prayer and I began. The words just flowed as the Lord gave me utterance and within an hour all ten were done and were to be aired after the 8.00 am news daily.

Next was the TV broadcast. We went in and searched for the religious department and eventually found the lady in charge and told her about the wonderful healings we had seen Jesus do in Malawi and asked her if she would like to interview us.

'I don't want to interview you,' she replied, 'I want to come with my cameraman and film these healings taking place.'

'Done,' I responded smiling, telling her the day and time.

'We will be ready and waiting.'

What a wonderful day it was, far better than sitting by a waterfall!

We then bought the five bicycles, five megaphones and twenty Bibles, all at a good discount on such a large order.

On Sunday we picked them up and took them to our final crusade of this trip and they filmed the preaching of the gospel, the people accepting Jesus as Lord and Saviour and then moved the cameras close in for the healings. I prayed for each person right through to a complete healing. Within a minute or two each person was able to testify of their healing. I then went on to the next person and the same happened until each one was

New church planted from the Bicycle Ministry

Princess thanks the Lord for the megaphone which has been used to plant a church of 150 people under some trees outside her village

healed and the camera had caught it all. Blind eyes were opened, the lame walked, arthritic hands opened up, and all sorts of healings. It was wonderful.

This broadcast was so popular that they had to re-show it at least three times due to popular demand. That is God. That is the way He demonstrates to a whole nation that He alone is God. There is no other

Ghana 2004

Another time, when the Lord moved in unexpectedly, was in Tokoradi, Ghana. We were supposed to give a customary visit to the Queen of Tokoradi, but she had been delayed and we could not wait any longer as we had a crusade to get to. As we left her residence, she arrived by car and wound down her window. We shook hands and, seeing there was no time to speak, I invited her to the crusade the following morning and she graciously accepted. Next morning she arrived and heard my message, 'Rise up to your full potential and calling in Christ.' She got excited about the message and immediately asked me to speak on the local radio programme *Politics and Christianity* between 1.00 pm and 2.00 pm.

We went to the Radio Station and were interviewed on how to rise up to the potential and calling that Christ has on our lives as Christians, rather than letting foreigners and other religions take control of the land. It was a challenging interview and I challenged the people to receive Jesus as Lord and to rise up and live up to the standards of the Bible and the Lord would then raise them up as leaders. I was then asked a very difficult question that I knew nothing about and I prayed. As I opened my mouth, wisdom came out, as God Himself put the words in my mouth, which amazed me when I played back the broadcast later.

As we walked back through the town, we could hear many talking about this lunchtime broadcast on the streets and realized yet again that the Lord had moved and had challenged the people.

Pakistan

'Oh Lord, give me faith to go! If You do not want me to go, please stop me now.' I left the check-in line at the airport, then stepped back in. 'It's the wrong time to go to Pakistan, I don't want to go, I want to come home alive, Lord,' I called out again.

Then I heard Him speak, 'I have called you and I will not forsake you.'

I went.

In Pakistan I was collected and headed for Sialkot. I was given Pakistani dresses to wear all the time. I had to travel with my face covered and I was not allowed out of the car. I was invited to speak at the largest Anglican cathedral in Sialkot. It went well. We then headed for a village and walked through handfuls of rose petals into a large courtyard of several hundred people. I preached the gospel to today's situation; the people responded and got excited. Soon more and more people came; the balconies of the surrounding houses filled up, then the roofs filled up with people as Jesus healed the sick. Suddenly two people born deaf and dumb were healed and repeated English words after me and everyone exploded into praise to God. The joy was so ecstatic that we all began to jump and dance for joy. No one wanted to go home and as I left for the next meeting, the children ran beside us to the end of the village. We had seen over 300 conversions on this one day.

Next day the same thing happened. A Muslim walking past the church suddenly got healed on the street of lung problems suffered for eight years. And, hearing us preach Jesus, he came straight in shouting, 'Who is this Jesus? I want to meet this Jesus who has just healed me.' He then testified how he had hardly been able to breathe for eight years, but that a few moments ago he heard the name of Jesus and was healed! He accepted Jesus right there and then. (This caused much excitement and resulted in many invitations to preach in more villages.)

We spent two days training pastors and evangelists and

anointed thirty to go out to the villages and then went to Lahore for the three-day crusade. The crusade welcomed me with fireworks and had closed off two streets for the conference, as I would not pay for a hall. I gave the gospel and thirty-two people responded to Jesus.

Next morning at 5.30 am the Lord spoke and said, 'You have preached the gospel, now get out.' Never had the Lord spoken to me like that. There was an urgency about it that had to be obeyed promptly. I would have to let people down. I went to breakfast. They put on the news. The US embassy had just been blown up, and more churches burnt down. All public transport in Lahore had already stopped.

We phoned to cancel the crusade and the pastor understood. We then headed straight out of Lahore and drove round the outskirts to meet the highway. Pastor Shakeels, who had tried to join us, was stuck on the outskirts, when the local transport had stopped. We picked up the smiling pastor, very relieved to see that we had made it out of Lahore safely, and drove back to Sialkot. As we left the last of the sprawling suburbs there was a large army of lorries driving to Lahore and horse and donkey carts trotting out of Lahore. I noticed a little donkey trotting flat-out with a driver standing on the cart behind him, reins in the left hand and a mobile phone to his ear with the right hand. 'I can guess what he is saying', I said, 'Yes, we have made it out of Lahore!'

The next day, Friday the 3rd March 2006, Pakistanis had planned for the demonstrations at the visit of George Bush, causing all the Christians to fast and pray for the situation. God answered and the day went amazingly peacefully, so much so that I was allowed to preach at a house church where 200 people squashed into the courtyard of a house.

We also then accepted the invitations of the villages and visited three each day, until we came home. Everywhere there was excitement, healings and response to Jesus. Huge welcome banners, chalk showing the way down narrow alleys, rose petals floating down on me from the rooftops and then up to seven garlands of roses put round my neck as I entered the crowds of villagers waiting to hear the Word from God. I thanked them for the welcome and the garlands and I said, 'But only One Person is worthy of such honour,' and I took off the garlands and placed them on the cross of Jesus and said in a loud voice, 'Now let us welcome Jesus.'

Clapping and response echoed out and they got more and more excited as I shared how much Jesus loved them, what He has done for us on the cross and what He still wants to give us today. I then prayed for the sick and the sick were healed and testified to the reality and healings of Jesus in our midst. Many accepted Jesus. They did not care that as Christians they would only get the road sweepers' jobs, and be denied education and many things. They had Jesus and Jesus is everything. The hunger for Jesus was greater than I have ever seen and I believed I was seeing revival break out.

After the church services, we would go to a home to eat. We would enter a bare room with cushions only round the walls and sit down on them on the floor. They would then bring in a tablecloth, put it on the floor and then the food came in whereupon we would all eat from the same dishes. The head of the house would then break up the chapattis and give us each a piece to scoop the food into our mouths. Everything reminded me of Jesus' Last Supper as nothing has changed in Pakistan in 2,000 years. They dress the same, live the same and have the same culture as when Jesus walked this earth; what a privilege to be there!

On Sunday morning, a burnt Bible inside a bag was found on the church steps where I was to speak, but we took no notice and just carried on. Even the Muslim guarding us with a gun responded to Jesus and joined us in the sinners' prayer from outside the church. One man testified of a healing from TB of seven years when we prayed for him the week before, and he brought the doctor's evidence of healing with him. Two more deaf and dumb were healed; strokes, chests and sore limbs all instantly healed.

To me this is village revival and yet another demonstration that the Lord is not just wanting to save groups of people here and there, but whole villages, cities, countries and nations.

Ghana 2005

It's March 2005 and we have to travel hundreds of miles by local minibus taxi to the far north. At the River Delta we have to cross the river, but we have missed the boat. We therefore hire a canoe. They collect the engine, tie it onto the canoe and we get in with our cases. There is a lot of water in the canoe and a young boy is scooping out the water.

'Don't worry,' the owner says, 'as long as we keep scooping out the water, the canoe won't sink.'

He is right and an hour later we land on the other side at exactly the same time as the boat we missed. Two of our team leap into the shallow water to race to the waiting buses to get us seats before they are all gone, while we puff behind with our cases. Well, at least we get on. I have to sit on the radiator for the next eight hours, while the others sit on the bus steps, but at least that was better than sitting on the luggage rack with our cases or waiting for the next bus tomorrow.

We bump over red gravel roads through typical African bush veldt, arriving totally red with dust, so that I cannot even put a comb through my fringe. At a small town we are to change buses, but there are no more buses that night. Eventually a Muslim, to whom we are very grateful, invites us to stay at his home.

At 6.00 am next morning we get our connecting bus to Wa, but this bus breaks down a couple of times, getting us to Wa at 6.00 pm in the evening. We are collected by the Pastor, taken to his home and given a bucket of water to wash ourselves, hair and clothing in, and I am shown to my room with a bed and a light that worked. What relief! I open a tin of baked beans, eat it and go to sleep.

Next morning I wake up sweating in 40° heat, feeling quite exhausted. I mean, all this way for three small villages! I decide it's better to pray, than dwell on human feelings. 'Lord,' I cry out. 'I command in the authority of the powerful name of Jesus, that every evil spirit bow the knee today in all three villages and I claim all three villages for Jesus to day, in Jesus' name, and I claim that three churches be planted today in Jesus' name.'

With exhaustion and sheer determination, I cry out to the Lord a little longer to be filled to the brim with His Holy Spirit, with His power to do His work today. I wipe my tears, take my bags and join the rest outside.

An hour later we arrive at the first village of 300 people. There is actually a church building there, but it has been closed for ten years, when the whole village became Muslims. I preach the Fall of Man and what God did about it by sending His Son Jesus to die on the cross to set us free from sin and death, to heal our bodies and to give us eternal life.

'Anyone sick here?' I ask and nearly get bombarded by sick people.

'Stand back,' I tell them. 'I just want one or two very sick people first.'

A lady who had a paralysed arm and crippled hand and fingers for ten years comes forward. I pray and simply watch as Jesus opens those fingers, moves her wrist, opens her elbow and then for the first time in ten years she can raise her hands above her head.

'This is the power of Jesus at work; this is because Jesus is alive and active. He is our living God and all we need to do is to receive Him as our personal Lord and Saviour. Who would like to receive Jesus as Lord and Saviour right now?'

Every single hand goes up, including the chief's. What joy it is to lead them through the sinners' prayer and to watch as each one receives Jesus as their Lord and Saviour.

I then pray for the rest of the sick and Jesus heals many more that morning, causing ecstatic joy and great excitement. I am asked to re-dedicate the church and pray over a couple of people to care for it and all the 300 people are excited to have church every week from this moment on.

We go to the next village. No church there; in fact they have no idea who Jesus is. It is a small village, but again after a few healings forty-nine people accept Jesus as Lord and Saviour and also want our team to plant a church there.

The third village is the biggest, around 600 people and as everyone turned up, we have to change our venue to the open air, under large mango trees. They stood round in a large circle, and welcomed us with a traditional dance, to drums and interesting looking music makers. The men would lift the women up and throw them up into beautiful leaps into the air. On landing, the dancers would prance in slow motion, lifting their heels right up to their seats, three dancers doing it at once, giving the appearance of prancing deer. It was beautiful to watch.

Next it was my turn to share with them the history of the Fall of Man, when we gave the world and ourselves over to Satan in exchange for the Knowledge of Good and Evil. I showed how evil had caused so much hardship, suffering, sickness and pain. Without God we were fallen human beings, just like the fallen angels, helpless to help ourselves out of many of the problems that life faces us with. Well, they all identified with that, as they were all living in dire poverty. They lived in mud huts with flat mud roofs, and ate from whatever game they could catch and vegetables they could grow. Clothing was scarce; some only owned the clothing on their bodies. If these people were ever sick, they could not afford doctors and there were simply no hospitals in that area at all. They either died or got well and that was that!

'But,' I went on 'God loved the world so much that He did something about this too. He sent His only Son Jesus to undo what the devil did to us, by becoming the perfect sacrifice for our sin. He took our sin upon Himself and died on the cross, went down to Hell, took the keys of death and hell back from the devil, then rose from the dead in total and complete victory over every sin, every sickness, every demon, every curse and over every evil thing and then ascended to heaven where He sits at the right hand of God in the heavenly places. As a result, when we turn from sin and the devil and accept what Jesus did for us on the cross, accepting Jesus into our hearts as Lord and Saviour, He will indeed come right into our very hearts, filling us with His forgiveness, love, joy, peace and presence. He will then cause us to live in a new victory in Him over all the power of the enemy and will also give us back what Adam and Eve had before they sinned, eternal life. Jesus has given us a second chance and He is alive right now and here right now in the spirit realm.'

They screamed with delight.

'If you want to receive Him in to your heart as your personal Saviour, put up your hand right now.'

Every hand went up.

'Say this prayer:

> Dear Lord,
> Thank You for dying on the cross to save us from sin. Please forgive me where I have sinned against You in thought, in word, in deed, in things I have left undone. Thank You, Jesus, for forgiving my sin – please come into my heart as my Lord and Saviour. Thank You, Jesus. Amen.'

After that I prayed for the sick in a general prayer as dusk was approaching. 'Put your hand on your sickness and pain and receive your healing now in Jesus' name.' Many people received their healing and we left them rejoicing and praising God. They wanted a church to be planted and invited the Wa team back next weekend to do so.

We drove back on the narrow dusty track with the sun

lowering over the bush veldt and the sweet smell of rain approaching us in dark clouds, the skies turned red. We passed a giant anthill palace, as I call them, almost fourteen feet high so I took a photo of it. It then began to rain, beautiful cool rain, causing clouds of steam to rise from the hot earth. What a beautiful ending to a wonderful day. *Jesus had done it yet again: 949 conversions in one day*. All three villages reached for Jesus.

We were given thirty minutes to bath with another bucket of water each, ate something fast – another tin of baked beans – and then went back to the bus station for our twenty-three-hour drive to our next destination.

We made it to the bus, loaded our cases on the roof and squashed into another overloaded bus. At least this time I managed an open window seat, so could enjoy the cooler night air.

Yes, evangelism is tough on the body, but days like this make it all worthwhile.

Prayer Camp

Twenty-eight long hours later including three breakdowns, we reach Bethlehem Prayer Camp near the Togo border. It is 9.00 pm. We are shown into a tin-roofed, mud building by candlelight and fall gratefully into bed in a very hot room. Next morning we are shown around many thatched, mud prayer-huts. This is where normally around 500 people stay when coming for the Lord to heal them. They fast for three days, attend two meetings a day and normally go home healed and the next group come in.

Jericho

We are then taken to Jericho, a grassy area with a wide path round it. In the middle, I am shocked to see people chained to the trees.

'There are no mental asylums in Ghana,' Prophet Elijah

explains. 'The mentally deranged, demon-possessed and mur-
derers are sent to prayer camps. We have to chain them. They
are dangerous; some will kill everyone they see.'

'So why do you chain them here?' I ask.

'You see this path?' he explains, 'twice a day all 500 visitors
come here. They march around Jericho seven times praying
twice a day and this causes the demons to leave!'

'You mean,' I ask, 'that the demons are so afraid of praying
Christians, that, as the people can't run because of the chains, the
demons run out of the people?'

'Yes, then they are free and can go home,' he explains simply.

Here I am left struggling with my theology a bit but, after
watching Elijah free a couple of these people, and having heard
their powerful testimonies that evening, my faith begins to rise
more and more to the power of prayer and the wonderful power
of God. Within between three days and a maximum of four
weeks, these demon-possessed, deranged, mad people were
totally and completely delivered, set free and healed to go home
as sane normal people!

'Elijah, I would rather be chained to a tree for four weeks than
spend a lifetime in a mental asylum in the West, with tablets to
merely subdue the symptoms, if I had the misfortune to be one of
them.'

Elijah has already built the Bible School classrooms, and
has fifty evangelists waiting to do Bible School, but is trusting
God to send the actual study materials somehow. So, when I tell
him that I have the Bible School notes to give him, he dances
around thanking God for answering his prayer and, by the
afternoon, I find myself teaching the first lesson of Step Out in
Faith Bible School to fifty eager students in their newly built
classroom.

Hugh Bettles also joins us here from Liberia. He has planted
the Bible School and Bicycle Ministry there and David Botchway
has done the same in Togo and we all return to Accra together.
Altogether, another six Bible Schools are planted on this trip.

Bethlehem Prayer Camp: hundreds march round Jericho seven times, twice a day, praying for demonic people who are chained to trees and for their own sicknesses

Sawing off chains from a demon-possessed man delivered and set free by Jesus

The USA

This trip to Ghana did take its toll on us. The journey from Wa to near the Togo border took twenty-eight hours with three bus breakdowns, a few hours' sleep and straight into a three-day crusade complete with baptising all the new Christians who responded, the day after, in the river. I then had diarrhoea and heatstroke together. By the time I arrived back in England I had typhoid fever and landed up in hospital.

'I am sorry, but you can't go to the USA in this condition,' the doctor said.

'But I must,' I said, 'I have been invited to speak on International TV.'

I had lost eight kilos in weight, but at least the high temperatures were down to normal due to the drips, so after a week I was able to come home to bed.

Only a few days to get well. I did not get out of bed until the day before I flew and ate my first full meal. The next morning I was up at 3.30 am. My husband reluctantly took me to the bus station and by 8.30 am I was taking off in the plane. By the time we reached the USA the Lord had entirely healed me. My friends picked me up at the airport and we bought two megaphones for Africa on the way to Voice Ministries.

Voice Ministries is a 24/7 prayer house run by Bob Deering and a wonderful team of godly people. I spent most of the next day, Monday, in the prayer house and early on Tuesday morning, Bob drove me to LeSea Broadcasting TV Network, South Bend, Indiana.

We entered a very spacious and beautiful reception area, collected our visitors' badges from the reception desk and were led into a comfortable well decorated lounge. There I saw a familiar bowl of fruit I had seen on TV and could now actually touch it to see if it was real or not! Then one of the interviewers, whom I also recognized, gave me a brief introduction, then to the make-up area, where I had a professional make-up 'do' to my face for TV.

Next down a hall into the biggest TV studio I had ever seen. 'Wait here,' I was told.

I looked around wondering, 'How did I get here?'

I looked across the large studio where the first guest was seated ready for the broadcast. Suddenly I saw the book that I had written *Dare to Enter His Presence* shown close-up on the TV screen as feature book and the interviewer introducing the show. 'Today we will be speaking to the author of *Dare to Enter His Presence* and she will be sharing with us how to come into the presence of God.'

My mind raced. 'So someone sent my book here? Is this why they invited me? I'd better watch closely so I get into the thread of the show, so I know what to say.'

After the introduction, the news, and feed the hungry clips, it was my turn. 'Lord, help me,' I whispered.

They showed me where to sit and I sat down. I prayed silently in tongues. Then we went live. They introduced me, I smiled and then the first question. As I opened my mouth the Lord's anointing just filled my whole being. I became more alive, excited, animated. The words just flowed out. I shared how to come into the presence of God with passion using the tabernacle prayer, then I was able to share what happens when one really comes to know God in prayer and how this alone opens the way into God's work. I shared how God began the ministry He had given me in Kenya with the miracle of the instant healing of the three blind ladies and the other 240 healings I saw at that conference. I was then thanked for sharing with them and was shown back to the lounge. They were pleased with the show and invited me back next year.

Dare to Enter His Presence remained feature book for the week and in the top ten for the month. Someone from Voice Ministries had sent them my book and somehow, out of the many they looked at, mine was chosen. When one serves God He does so much more than one can ever think or imagine, for this broadcast went out worldwide to millions of people.

This is the God we serve. He gives victory every time. The devil may attack you, and try to stop you from reaching your goal, as he tried to do to me, when he caused me to be so sick before coming to the USA. But we have to fight the devil. We have to be determined. That's when the Lord moves in and simply makes it happen. The more we serve the Lord, the more we need to pray. The bigger the ministry, the bigger the attacks from the devil get, but in prayer God alone takes us from level to level, from victory to victory and as we live out the powerful words of Scripture, the Lord will do the rest. He can use normal people like you and me to reach out to the uttermost parts of our earth.

As I think back, I remember being called as a riding instructor a 'walking textbook' because I studied horse books so much and put everything I learnt into practice on the horses I rode and for the pupils I taught. Yes, that's where I began.

'Lord,' I prayed, 'I would rather be known as a 'walking Bible' than a 'walking textbook'. I would rather be living Your Word and showing the power of Your wonderful Word to all I meet.'

I love the Lord so much. I love His Word so much, alive, living words of a loving and living God. Yes, He loves you so much that He sent His only Son for you.

God loves the world so much that He sends His Holy Spirit upon all who will receive Him and will go with us to the furthest and the most remote places, even to the smallest villages for just one simple reason, God's love. My victory is in Christ's love, their victory is in Christ's love, and your victory is in Christ's love. Let us all step out in faith together, let us take God's love to the ends of the earth. Let us move as one in Christ in the different directions and places God has for us, in the gifting He has gifted us with and the world will recognise Him by our love.

In John 17:20–26 Jesus prayed not only for His own disciples but for all who would believe in Him through their message:

> '*My prayer is not for them alone. I pray also for those who will believe in me through their message, that all of them may be one,*

Father, just as you are in me and I am in you. May they also be in us so that the world may believe that you have sent me. I have given them the glory that you gave me, that they may be one as we are one: I in them and you in me. May they be brought to complete unity to let the world know that you sent me and have loved them even as you have loved me. Father, I want those you have given me to be with me where I am, and to see my glory, the glory you have given me because you loved me before the creation of the world. Righteous Father, though the world does not know you, I know you, and they know that you have sent me. I have made you known to them, and will continue to make you known in order that the love you have for me may be in them and that I myself may be in them.'   (NIV)

Jesus is talking to you and me through these precious words of Scripture right now. This scripture was written for us, right where we are, right into our time sphere right now. We are the only ones who can reach our own generation. If we don't, no one else will.

You are a life

Only once, my friend, in the creation of the world
Do you have the chance to exist
Only once, my friend, in the History of Mankind
Can you contribute your special part.

Awake my friend, how special life is
Every day you are alive in this world
Awake my friend, you have a life to live
And a part, that only you can fulfil.

You are created, my friend, by God on High
To find your place in His love
You are created my friend, in your life to find
God's purpose in life to fulfil.

And your life, my friend, looks to eternity
By the life you live on this earth
And your life, my friend, as you serve our God
Ends with victory in Christ's love.

There is no higher calling, no nobler a task, no greater gift that
we can give our God than to serve our fellow man with Christ's
love. Nothing else can we take to Heaven, other than those we
have led to Christ.

Will you step out in faith with me, to go to those special
people He has called you to? It matters not how many or how
few, but it proves our love and obedience to our Lord.

Let us together cause a smile to come upon our Father's face.
Let us receive the words of Jesus, deep within our hearts, and
Jesus will come with us, wherever we may go.

Jesus prayed:

*'O righteous Father! The world has not known You, but I have
known You; and these have known that You sent Me.'*

(John 17:25)

We know Jesus whom the Father has sent.

*'And I have declared to them Your name, and will declare it, that
the love with which You loved Me may be in them, and I in them.'*

(John 17:26)

For me walking close to Jesus is the best part of evangelism. This
is even better than seeing the healing miracles where you
actively feel the beauty of the love and healing flow through
your very being into that precious person whom God loves so
much and is healing. It is living in the beauty of His glorious
presence that makes you feel so complete in Him.

Jesus, You sent the love that the Father had for You to be

within us! Jesus, You come and live in us, just as the Father lived in You! As Jesus in John 17:23 says:

> *'I in them and you in me. May they be brought to complete unity to let the world know that you sent me and have loved them even as you have loved me.'*
>
> (NIV)

What more could we ever need than to know Jesus and His love day by day, and for His love to live in us? It is His love that transforms us; it is His love that fills us with so much energy. It is His love that enables us to step out in faith and go, and it is His love that gives us the victory. Our victory is in Christ's love. Let us step out in faith together!

Bethlehem Prayer Camp: baptizing new believers

A prayer for salvation or recommitment

Dear Lord Jesus, I come to You as I am. Please forgive me, when I have sinned in thought, in word, in deed, in things left undone, and please come into my life as my Lord and Saviour. Thank You, Lord. Amen.

A prayer for baptism in the Holy Spirit

Please baptise me in Your Holy Spirit that I can be more effective for You. Thank You, Lord. Amen.

Now just receive Him. He will also enable you to pray more effectively daily, and read your Bible with more understanding. Join a church or Christian fellowship and tell someone of your new commitment to the Lord.

If you should require further prayer, you are welcome to contact me (see p. 191 for details).

May God bless you, may His hand be upon your life as you live out your Christian life day by day, allowing the Lord to guide you and help you live it out. May He strengthen you and fill you with His perfect love, joy, and peace. Amen.

A thought on serving the Lord effectively

It's not how many hours we spend in prayer
but the degree that we know Him.

It's not how much we can do for the Lord
but the amount of love that we serve Him with.

It's not the size of the anointing we have
but the degree we die to self to release Him.

It's not what *we* can do for the Lord
but what *He* can do through us.

Books by Suzanne Pillans

Dare to Follow
This book is the story of Suzanne's walk with God and reveals something of His faithfulness to those willing to follow Him wholeheartedly.

'I believe this book will challenge and inspire you to go further with God than you have ever gone. I hope that it leads you into an adventure of faith yourself.'
(Clive Corfield, Sovereign Ministries)

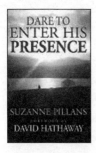

Dare to Enter His Presence
(feature book in the USA TV *Harvest Show*)
This book is full of quotations from the Bible. Suzanne Pillans uses them to teach us about prayer, or rather, shares with us what she has learnt from her deep knowlege of the words of the Bible. She is passionate about our need to approach Christ ever more closely, to commune with Him, and ever increase our love for Him and our obedience to His teaching. She shares what this closeness to God has meant in her own life; a life of healing and anointing in His own name, and following His direction. She teaches that God has made us wonderful promises, and we need to come close to Him, so that we can claim these promises.

The Biblical Approach to Basic Horsemanship
This book is written for riding instructors, horse trainers and horse lovers who want to approach horsemanship in the way that God intended us to.

For the rider. An easy to understand approach to sound practical horsemanship for the beginner or horse owner and those interested in this ideal approach to their riding.

For the Christian. A book showing how God can be part of horsemanship and how to use the Bible as a basis for other sports along with daily living.

Teaching Video DVDs of TV Broadcasts by Suzanne Pillans

1. *Introduction to Ministry* (free with any order, on request)
2. *The Power of the Cross*
3. *Do Not Limit God*
4. *The Kingdom of God is at Hand*
5. *Rise Up to Your Call*
6. *The Gift of Righteousness*
7. *True Freedom*
8. *The Lord's Prayer*
9. *The Power of Prayer*
10. *Authority in Prayer*
11. *Filled without Limit*
12. *Equipped to Serve*
13. *The Spiritual Realm*
14. *The Anointing*
15. *To Step Out in Faith*
16. *The Blessing of Obedience*
17. *Village Evangelism*

These can be purchased individually for £5.00 each,
or in groups of eight of your choice for £30.00 per set.

Contact details

For more information or for ordering books write to:
    Suzanne's Ministries
    Step Out in Faith
    Standlake Ranch, Downs Road
    Standlake, Witney
    Oxfordshire OX28 7UH

or

    Tel: 01865 300099
    Email: wpillans@aol.com
    Website: www.standlakeranch.co.uk
        www.suzannesministries.co.uk

Standlake Ranch with an inner-city camp

Meeting hall at Standlake Ranch

Would you would like to recieve our free DVD
with *Healing, Entering His Presence, Don't Limit God,* and the
Bicycle Ministry, plus newsletters of our evangelistic trips?
Please send us your name and address to:
Standlake Ranch, Downs Road, Standlake
Witney, Oxfordshire OX29 7UH, England
or email to:
wpillans@aol.com
and we will gladly send this to you.

We hope you enjoyed reading this New Wine book.
For details of other New Wine books
and a range of 2,000 titles from other
Word and Spirit publishers visit our website:
www.newwineministries.co.uk